THE ATTENTION BUSINESS

Proven Ways to Grow Your Business Using
Social Media Marketing, Google, Facebook,
Amazon, Twitter, YouTube and LinkedIn

THE ATTENTION BUSINESS: PROVEN WAYS TO GROW YOUR BUSINESS USING SOCIAL MEDIA MARKETING, GOOGLE, FACEBOOK, AMAZON, TWITTER, YOUTUBE, AND LINKEDIN

ISBN-13: 9781503298442

ISBN: 1503298841

Contents

Who Is This Book For?

Do you want to harness the power of Google, Apple, Amazon, Facebook, Twitter, YouTube and LinkedIn, and get them to bring traffic directly to you?

Do you feel **overwhelmed** by all the tasks involved in Social Media and online marketing?

Google, Twitter, Facebook, YouTube, Amazon, LinkedIn – you know they're all powerful channels, but there's so much work! How do you know where to start?

Do you want to create a plan for Social Media which will make it easier, save you time and increase effectiveness 10-fold?

Do you want to turbocharge your business, its visibility and its sales with Social Media?

Do you want to know the *3 Critical Factors for Success* in online marketing?

Do you feel you are not up to speed with Social Media and online marketing?

Do you want to find a *system*, a long-term system for bringing qualified sales leads to you?

Do you want to learn practical techniques for succeeding with Facebook, Twitter, LinkedIn and YouTube?

Do you want to know the best way to work across Facebook, LinkedIn, Twitter, YouTube, Google, iTunes and Amazon with the least possible effort?

Do you want to know about *"The Inbound Marketing Revolution"* and how it could lower your cost of sales leads by *67%?*

Do you feel your own Social Media marketing efforts are random, haphazard and not producing results?

Do you want to learn simple analysis techniques like MDIs and ICPs, which will simplify and focus your efforts?

Do you want to be seen as an expert in your field, with enhanced credibility and reputation?

If the answer to any of these questions was "yes", then The Attention Business can answer a lot of questions for you. At the very least you should understand where online marketing and Social Media marketing are going at this time, and how you can take advantage of that with only a moderate amount of effort.

However, in addition to explaining to you just how big this marketing opportunity is, I will to go into as much of the detail as I *reasonably* can about how you should make your plans, and implement your marketing activities. I've tried to keep this book to the point, so there is a lot more information on my website (for free) that I will refer to throughout.

www.TheAttentionBusiness.com

Within reason (and while trying not to bore the pants off my readers) I will include as much detail as I can. As I will say later, it is far more important **_what_** you do, rather than **_how_**. It's about decisions, planning and execution – and how to avoid getting overwhelmed and bogged down. The how is the **_execution_** part of your campaign, and it's important; but if you got your decisions and your plan wrong in the first place, it doesn't matter how good your execution is. So the **_what_** comes before the **_how_**.

This book is about planning, going in the right direction and knowing what you are doing. It talks about how you should go about the work, but necessarily a lot of the detail is included at my site, www.TheAttentionBusiness.com. If all the details were included you would be wading around in a book 1000 pages long. Still, it will be obvious as you progress in the book that there are plenty of specific techniques and resources in this book which can be invaluable to you, and save you huge amounts of time, frustration and head-scratching. On my website I have created a lot more resources and lists of links which you can access at any time as you read through the book.

Before we get started, though, I need to let you have some background about why Social Media Marketing, and Inbound Marketing really ARE a revolution. I started in online marketing and building online communities for my target markets way back in 1998.

There have been some big changes in online marketing in that time, but it is this latest revolution that is really opening up the power of the Internet Giants like Google, Facebook and YouTube to the small business and the little guy. In short, this what the Internet should be all about. This revolution is empowering individuals, and allowing free rein to each and every marketer, regardless of financial resources.

That is what inspired me to write this book. I believe passionately in small business, start-ups and in people building strong, prosperous communities by building their own enterprises. The game has changed in your favour! I want to empower as many small businessmen and women as I can to take advantage of this.

My Story: Why I Passionately Want to Share this Knowledge

When I began marketing online back in 1997, we could all see that the Internet was an incredibly powerful phenomenon, but we didn't really know how to make money out of it. Back then it was possible to build communities simply by building websites and user forums which our target market would want to look at two There were banner ads and one or two other innovations, but I was marketing for a start-up publisher of tech books, and we found that building communities was a highly cost-effective way of reaching our target market of programmers and software developers.

In the years that followed however, we went through the Dotcom Boom, when obscene amounts of cash were thrown at building customer bases online. For some corporations, the tactic worked. Amazon burned billions of investors' money and destroyed half of the bookselling business in the US, Canada and the UK into the bargain, before it made a cent in profit. On paper, Amazon's first few years were an exercise in value destruction. Yet who would deny that Amazon has always provided a great service and innovated constantly? The "land-grab" of customers worked for Amazon, even if it cost billions.

Other hugely funded online ventures crashed and burned one after the other.

Perhaps foolishly, I kept up my own online businesses, selling books and training systems on the Internet, and over the space of ten years or so I watched as key markets for goods online came to be dominated by one or two enormous and well-funded players.

I had a great team around me, however, and through great service, low prices and constant innovations in service, we found we could hold our own. We were increasing sales again in the last few year, right up until I decided to sell out in 2012. I had diversified, automated, squeezed out costs, cut staff numbers (while improving service), yet I still found I could hardly make any money out of the stuff I was selling.

It was my accountant who told me that my business was strangling me, and that I should get out. At the same time, my oldest child had been suffering with complex health issues for a year already and we'd had some dire conversations with his doctors. I did the only thing I could reasonably do, and sold out.

(I have to say my son is much better, and his conditions are now well controlled. He has started university and has taken up sports once more, which is quite something since for two years he was not well enough even to go to school. Chalk another one up for perseverance...)

During my long struggle to "crack" the secret of low-cost online marketing, I tried so many different techniques, and for some of the time one or other of these methods was very cheap and effective. Email marketing was superb before the spammers ruined it; pay-per-click was cheap and highly effective for a while; search engine optimization brings in torrents of traffic if you get it right, but the traffic can disappear just as quickly as it came.

After selling my businesses I spent a lot of time learning and educating myself on the latest techniques in online marketing, especially in Social Media, which has been evolving rapidly all this time. Content marketing has also arisen as an extremely effective way of promotion and branding. From there I went further and further into the opportunities presented by big ecommerce platforms like Amazon, eBay and Apple's iTunes, as well as YouTube, Facebook and the rest.

It became obvious to me that the really big players on the Internet were making it easier and easier for me to get involved.

At the same time I was asked by the Prince's Trust PRIME charity to give my time to mentor and teach entrepreneurship in the over 50s age group. HRH Prince Charles recently invited me to his London residence at Clarence House in recognition of my work, which is a nice touch. PRIME aims at the over-50s, and these are often people with huge experience and expertise. They have so much to offer, but so many of them find the idea of marketing and self-promotion daunting. In fact they speak of it as some kind of "black art". I came to realise that professional marketers have spent years creating a kind of mystique around marketing. I spent more and more of my time helping and advising entrepreneurs and small businesses in online marketing and ecommerce techniques.

I discovered something which is in fact quite obvious. Small businesses, especially micro-businesses and start-ups, don't have a lot of spare cash. If they can do things in a clever, low-cost way, they certainly will. And of course the Internet offers cheaper, easier and more effective ways of doing all sorts of things, from accounting and bookkeeping to legal services, virtual assistants, payment systems, and so on.

It also offers cheaper and easier selling channels, in the shape of marketplaces like Amazon, eBay and many smaller, specialist arenas. Why bother with the old ways of selling products, when you can do your market testing on Amazon Marketplace? You can see what products and price-points work best before you even start! You can access a huge market from day one. And since you are selling direct, you can keep most of the retail price.

If you want, Amazon will even look after the warehousing and delivery side of things!

I came across a lady called Sue who has designed and created a wall clock which makes it easy to tell the time. It is aimed at children who are learning to tell the time, and the clock is bought by schools and by families.

Sue had some clocks manufactured in China, and decided to test the market by selling on Amazon Marketplace. It's a great product and quickly became the number one selling clock on Amazon UK.

After six months of sales rising way beyond her expectations, Sue had the decision of how to expand the sales yet further. She identified that she could sell a lot more to schools – that was her first option. She also noticed that she was getting some orders from the US and Canada, even though the product wasn't listed on Amazon in those countries. Sue faced the choice of phoning schools, visiting them and selling the clocks on the one hand; or on the other hand shipping clocks to an Amazon warehouse in the US and allowing Amazon to sell the clocks for her in North America. Amazon make it very easy for her to do this. Not only that but the products automatically rate high on Google and other searches.

In short, Amazon have made it so easy for a seller like Sue. She has no experience of online marketing, logistics, ecommerce, online payment security and the rest. However, she has a good product at a good price and Amazon have made it incredibly easy for her. Amazon WANT people like Sue, and they want to sell their products. In fact Amazon NEED people like Sue.

I could go on with so many examples, but the bottom line is this: Imagine for a second that Sue were not able to sell her clocks through Amazon. What would I advise her to do? Why, I would advise her to sell them on eBay.

Imagine further that all the small and micro-businesses like Sue and her clocks were **excluded** from Amazon, but were selling on eBay instead. It's not difficult to see what would happen. eBay would take a huge slice of Amazon's business. eBay would in effect be able to harness all that creativity and the ingenuity of all those entrepreneurs, small businesses, micro-businesses and individuals. Those thousands of "little guys" are be an unstoppable force.

Amazon wants that unstoppable force of small traders and entrepreneurs working for Amazon. eBay wants that mass of traders working for eBay. Amazon and eBay are in deadly competition. That's why they're making it easier and easier for the little guy to succeed.

Sue with her clocks has been creative and ingenious, and that is why Amazon wants and needs her. In fact the **Internet** wants her. The **Internet** wants creative and ingenious people like Sue.

The Internet is about reach and easy access to the mass of huge populations. But that mass of people is not only the mass of consumers and buyers, which is what the Big Guys thought ten or fifteen years ago. The Internet is about the mass of creative, ingenious people.

The Internet is about the millions of creators, traders, sellers and experts out there; and the Internet Giants like Google, Facebook, YouTube, Amazon, iTunes, Twitter, LinkedIn and eBay are well aware of that fact.

After years as a small businessman, and then some more years advising, helping and mentoring small businesses, I am constantly overwhelmed by the creativity, determination and belief of these people. I also know that there are millions more knowledgable folks out there who would like to express their creativity and ingenuity. They all have so much to offer.

But having something to offer isn't enough.

The difficult part in starting out on your own is grabbing people's ***attention*** – letting people know you what you offer and what you can do for them. We are all in The Attention Business.

Like it or not, we are all in The Attention Business.

And in business, as we all know, we can't just go through the motions - we have to perform. No one expects to succeed in business by doing a half-baked job. The Attention Business is no different. We have to ***perform***, and that is what this book is about.

The "What" and the "Why" Come First – The "How" Comes Later

In any business guide or book or video, we are all tempted to rush ahead and see how it is done. For instance, when it comes to online marketing with Social Media or blogs or video or promoting through Amazon – we are all looking for a "How-to", or a secret trick or technique.

Well, the world, and the Internet especially, are full of guides about how to do stuff. What is far more important is "What" you decide to do, and "How" you decide to do it.

As the name of this book suggests, this is primarily a book how to promote yourself online; but the first questions you need to answer are **_what_** you do, and **_why_**. Only then can you decide how to actually perform.

Decide what to do – plan what to do – learn how to do it. The **_what_** always comes before the **_how_**.

Think about it. When it comes to the "how" of online marketing, you can learn how to do it yourself; you pay someone else to do it; you can copy someone else's methods; or you can strive to do something exciting or unique. But if you're going to put in hours of learning and trial and error on say Facebook marketing or Google Adwords or optimizing your site for Google; or if you're going to spend hard-earned cash on getting someone to do this stuff, then you sure as hell better be doing the right thing in the first place.

Off the top of my head I'm sure can think of 40 or 50 online marketing methods you could use to promote your business. Let me try...

Facebook groups

Facebook ads

Facebook page

Twitter

Google optimization

Google Adwords

Google long-tail optimization

Google+

Blogging

Ezines

Forum posting

Video promo

YouTube embedded

YouTube search

Affiliate scheme

Ebooks

Free content

Email

Email list-building

Email auto-response

Partnerships

Yahoo Answers

LinkedIn profile

LinkedIn groups

Linkedin search

Facebook search

Local directories

Amazon Marketplace

Amazon freebies

Amazon search

Amazon ebooks

Expert publications

Banner ads

Trade-specific sites

Testimonials and endorsements

Link building

Online PR

Online press articles

iTunes Podcasts

Local ezines

Review sites

Content marketing

Inbound marketing

Website

And on it goes... I haven't even started with *off*line methods of marketing yet. How many of these can you do and still make a good job of it? One? Four? Six maximum I would suggest.

And are you going to learn the how-to of five or ten marketing options before you begin? ***Of course not...*** So you have choices to make about ***what*** to do.

Just as every person is unique, every business is unique. Every business needs its own "marketing mix", not a prescribed formula. I often hear it said that this or that technique "has to be part of the marketing mix". Well... no it doesn't. Everything is open. Yes, it's a good idea to follow tried and tested formulas, but your business will be your unique little baby. And you will need to make the right decisions to make sure that your baby survives, thrives, and flourishes in the longer term. Treat it as your baby, and think hard about the decisions you make on behalf of your child. You want the best for your child don't you?

So research the online marketing techniques, and choose the right ones for you.

1. Choose Your Online Marketing Techniques Carefully – And Give Yourself the Best Possible Chance From the Start

This is undoubtedly the most important thing you will read in this book. So I will repeat myself:

CHOOSE CAREFULLY!

And when I say choose, I mean the choice of what marketing methods are going to fit in with what your business does, who your *ideal* customers, the *direction* your business is headed, the growth the speed of growth you want, and perhaps most importantly, **the kind of person you are**.

Choosing carefully means thinking through the ramifications of the different techniques available, and choosing the right one for you which will give you the best chances of success, given your own personal circumstances, particularly the resources you have at your disposal. By resources I mean money, but also time, manpower and skillset.

Marketing methods can require money, such as page advertising, Google Adwords, sponsorships and affiliate schemes. They can be time consuming, such as Facebook groups, Twitter and blogging. They can give instant results like advertising, Adwords and PR. They can be slow but long-lasting like link-building, blogging and SEO.

Most of us will try to hit a number of these methods as part of the marketing mix, but it is possible to do the job with only one method. I help a number of travel businesses with their marketing, and I recently networked with a lady (Larissa) who used only PR to market her business, and she did it herself.

One of the perks of being a travel agent is the fantastic free trips and cut-price holidays which you can take. Larissa wrote up and article with high quality photos every time she took one of these trips, and sent them to the local press. Soon she was getting regular articles in the local papers, who are always hungry for interesting articles especially if accompanied by eye-catching photos. The articles reference Larissa's business of course, and she gets enquiries from them.

That is all Larissa does in the way of marketing.

So you see, there are dozens of different methods of grabbing people's attention online. *The Attention Business* is all about choosing the right method for you, and then performing as perfectly as you can.

You quite often hear it said of entrepreneurs: "He was in the right place at the right time". People say that all the time as if it's all down to luck — but you can make your own luck by *choosing carefully, so that your marketing positions you in front of the right people at the right time.*

When choosing which online marketing method to pour your time and effort into, think where your business wants to be:

In the right place at the right time,

Reaching people who you KNOW are interested in what you are offering,

Reaching people who you KNOW will pay for what you're offering,

Reaching people who you KNOW can be profitable to you.

The interesting thing about these four aims of your marketing mix is that these are the EXACT SAME aims as the enormous Internet Giant corporations like Google, Facebook, Apple, Amazon and the rest. These firms have invested billions in reaching these people, right down to each micro-niche. They have ALREADY identified a ton of customers who are perfect for you.

And the best thing of the lot is this: Google, Amazon, Facebook, iTunes, YouTube, Twitter, LinkedIn – they all WANT to put you and your goods and services in front of those customers. So look for where your interests and markets coincide with the markets of the Internet Giants.

That's what modern Internet marketing is all about. It's about working with and exploiting these Internet Giants.

The other thing about choosing carefully should be more obvious. This is YOUR business, YOUR hard work, and YOUR money to be made - or lost. Friends, family and professional business advisers (especially professional business advisers) cannot tell you what you are going to love and hate about your business, and what you will find truly fulfilling.

For this reason remember: take advice - but this is YOUR decision, and only yours.)

The Latest Revolution in Online Marketing – And Why It Puts You in The Driving Seat

To give you an idea of the stupendous reach of *__just one__* Internet platform, consider this. By January 2014, 1.23 billion users were active on the Facebook website in a single month, and at that time 945 million of that total were identified as mobile users – using smartphones or tablets.

Facebook is not identified specifically as a marketing platform, although it has plenty of opportunities for the marketer, such as Facebook groups and paid Facebook ads. The importance of Facebook as an example of Social Media is its enormous reach, vast user numbers, and the fact that it is now very much a mobile medium, used on smartphones and tablets, rather than computers and laptops.

Let's just remind ourselves right now of an astonishing fact.

Barely 20 years after the beginning of the World Wide Web, we now have a situation where 80% of the human race has access to the Internet. That means we each of us have a connection, personally and directly, to 80% of the people on this planet, which is almost 6,000,000,000 people.

Despite what we might read in the news, the world is now in a period of unprecedented prosperity and abundance compared to any other era in human history. Combine that with the networked nature of the Internet, and we can see that the new markets are constantly opening up, especially for small businesses and even start-ups. Perhaps that's why more and more people are choosing to start their own business, and there are more buyers, more choices and more variety than ever before.

Now, let's add that unprecedented interconnectedness to the wide choice of Internet devices which have sprung up in the last few years. Ten years ago, the vast majority accessed the Internet from home or work computer, or possibly a laptop. As of 2014, most homes in your town or city will access the Internet from smart phones, tablets, computers, games consoles, Internet-enabled TVs and even their cars.

This astonishing situation means that if you have an effective web-presence you can be in front of your customers _**at virtually any time**_. You can be in their living room, on their TV, on their workstation, in their pockets, in their hands, with them on the train and even in their cars. Wherever those customers are, they can find you and interact with you in seconds.

But, but, but... Surely I could object at this stage that the amount of "noise" in the online world is just as big, if not bigger, than the opportunity. It can be almost impossible to make yourself heard online, can't it? Even getting found on a search engine can be very difficult task.

All that is true; *but things are now turning in your favour,* especially if you have a great web presence with a ton of interesting and engaging content.

You may have heard it said before that "content is king". It has become something of a cliché online; but like many clichés it is absolutely true.

Yes, Content is King.

Let me explain in step-by-step fashion why *Content really is King*.

1. An astonishing amount of web traffic and revenue is owned by a small number of properties which I will call the Internet Giants. These are for that same reason the biggest brands in the world right now. I am talking about Google, Apple, Facebook, YouTube, Amazon, LinkedIn, Twitter and then a bunch of what

we could call second rank online properties, which are still huge in their own right. The second rank operatives include Diggit, Reddit, Tumblr, Vimeo, DailyMotion and many, many more. These corporations are worth billions. The market value of their shares is stratospheric. We all know that. What do you suppose is the main strategic goal for all these Internet Giants? The number one goal for these Internet Giants is to maintain their positions for as long as they can; because their positions are more fragile than they appear.

2. When was the last time you, or anyone you know visited MySpace or Bebo? And yet it's only a few years since both of these properties were spoken of as rivals to Facebook. Yahoo was once the biggest deal on the Internet; then it was AOL. Things can change very quickly. That means that Facebook, Google, Amazon and the rest can see very clearly how fast their customers can desert them. It only takes one rival to have an edge, and win a decent share of the market, and immediately the position of any one of these Giants of the Internet Age will be under threat.

3. The reason the Internet Giants are so giant is that they have *so many people contributing to their networks*. Facebook is where every goes to network. eBay is the best auction site, with the most buyers and the most sellers. Amazon has the biggest and best marketplace and the most customer reviews.

Most people upload their videos to YouTube rather than another platform, and for that reason, most people **_search_** YouTube for videos. These Internet Giants make their money from their huge audiences; but at the same time, Google, Facebook, Twitter, iTunes and the rest **_rely on their vast audiences_** for engaging, surprising and inspiring content. Without the content of their contributors, these Internet Giants are nothing, and the vast majority of their content is provided by their users. The Internet Giants need you.

4. The Internet Giants have an insatiable desire for fresh, engaging content, and they increasingly look after users who are providing that useful, expert, engaging content. They can't get enough of it!

This is the reason why Content is King.

If you produce engaging, useful and expert content, and make it available on all the billions of devices, as text, photos, videos, presentations, podcasts and the rest, the Internet Giants want you. They want to help you and they will be cheering you on. They will make you visible and they will help to promote you to their millions and billions of users. They will target you at exactly the kind of people who are interested in what you offer.

Facebook has 1.35 BILLION active users each month.

YouTube shows 5 BILLION videos every day and ranks just behind Facebook in users.

Google+ has 345 million active users

Even the professionals' network LinkedIn boasts 343 million active users

(Statista.com)

There are no figures I know of in marketing that compare remotely to these; no TV station in history has come anywhere near. What's more all of these eyeballs are available to you at low- or no-cost! There has never been a better time to use digital marketing, and even if you feel you are "late to the game" it doesn't matter. And new game has begun, and you need to become a player.

The New Game in Digital Marketing: the Coalescence of Search Engine Optimization, Social Media, Content and Public Relations

Just to be clear what I mean here:

Search engine optimization (SEO) means a number of techniques to make your webpages rank higher on Google and other search engines. Traditionally, this has included gaining links from other websites, preferably high quality websites; having a good amount of relevant and frequently updated text; and having the right HTML structure to the pages.

Public relations are the activities around getting press and media coverage for your business.

Content marketing refers to putting useful blogs, videos, articles, podcasts, infographics or e-zines online to build your brand as an expert and to get people's attention and interest.

These three broad areas have grown up separately, but they are now starting to come together as a holistic idea. There is hot debate about this in world of SEO and PR in particular. Until recently they had no connections at all! The debate centres around this question: Can SEO, PR and content stand alone or have they become intrinsically linked?

Well, my response is – do we care? While the marketing industry is having the debate, we as business people and marketers can get on and exploit the opportunities.

Google updates always have some kind of impact on the industry, and the recent Panda update had far reaching effects, basically making it more difficult to fake good quality links, and downgrading sites with boring but SEO-friendly text. ***Key Fact: Google's Panda update has prioritized high quality, shareable content and it loves video.***

Quality, shareable content

Not so long ago link-building strategies (that is working to gain links to your site from other related and heavily trafficked sites) and a heavy use of keywords were the leading focus of SEO campaigns. That's changed.

Since the recent Panda changes to the Google relevancy algorithms, content has been elevated to a higher importance in the Google search results. This has shifted things to the advantage of the blog and article writers, video makers and podcasters. It also means an end to those boring web pages where the same phrases are repeated over and over, in favour of imaginative, genuine content.

As the Guardian newspaper says, it's about "creating quality content that people want to share."

Content, whether articles or blogs or video, needs to be:

Entertaining or useful

Shareable

It needs to be something that people will want to share.

How does Google know whether your material is shareable and high quality? That's where Social Media come in. Google highly rates content if it has been liked, shared, tweeted and watched. So you need to integrate your use of Social Media.

There are approximately 160 million blogs online and about five billion **hours** of video being watched every month on YouTube. That's not five billion videos, that's five billion **hours**, before we even consider videos embedded in people's sites and other video sites like Vimeo or DailyMotion.

You have an unparalleled, unprecedented opportunity to connect to consumers by creating compelling content and putting it out there. Make it shareable, and make it the kind of thing we all want to share. Think of those videos or clips or images that get shared by friends, then hundreds of friends, then thousands. That's called "going viral" and it's the holy grail of video marketing; and together with your subject area and keywords, it's how you'll get your video showing on page one of Google.

But you don't have to aim so high. After all, you don't want to get in front of any random eyeball on the Internet. You want to get in front of *your* target market. For a business-related video, you don't need that many views to rank well.

Another factor with videos, blogs and all manner of other posts online is frequency. If you can make high quality blogs or videos, and publish frequently, then your material will be found more often on Google. A recent study by Hubspot found that 56% of bloggers and YouTubers who posted once a gained sales leads. That rose to 92% for those who posted daily.

So you can see that Google, with its Panda Update, has brought SEO and Social Media Marketing together on the same track, along with content creation. If you get the content right, and spend time diligently distributing that content, it can result in a torrent of traffic for you – more than you can handle.

So how do you get it right? Let me start with three critical success factors.

Three Critical Success Factors in Social Media Marketing and Content Creation

The Three Critical Success Factors are:

Passion (or Love)

Trust

Expertise at Expertise (Not only being an expert, but looking like one)

I'll return to this may times throughout the book, but building that brand requires three main things, which I'll talk about in the following chapters:

Loving yourself, showing your passion and projecting the enthusiasm. This has to come through in your *performance*.

Establishing Trust and credibility.

Being an expert, at being an expert (hint: you don't have to be an expert to pull this off).

Love Yourself, Love What You Do - and Share the Love via Social Media

You see it's all very nice. After Love comes Trust – and no you haven't opened a romance novel by mistake! Love and Trust go together very naturally though.

Your business and your job are a major part of your life. It goes without saying. It gives you money, self-respect, satisfaction...

My daughter always tells me that three hours doing her homework assignment for Art is so much less work than doing 20 minutes for Physics for example. If you love what you're doing, and love the activities it involves, things will be much easier.

A 14-hour day spent working at something you enjoy will go much faster than six hours of something you think you OUGHT to enjoy.

We all know people, including some very successful people, who talk about the late evenings and weekends they have worked. However, ask yourself why they do this. Very often these people have more than enough money – but of course that's not why they do it. The truth is, most of these people do it because they LOVE THEIR WORK.

This love is a huge part of their success. Because they love their work, they are happy to work very hard on it; but more importantly, these people constantly project a passion and enthusiasm for what they do, which is infectious.

Love is a big part of success – and if you don't love what you're offering to your customers, how are you going to get them to love it?

Love Yourself

The reason to love what you do, is that you will find it so much easier to sell your business, your ideas and yourself if you have infectious enthusiasm.

The second part of "loving it" is loving yourself. Small business owners are, for the most part, selling **themselves**. You are THE central part of what the business is about. People will buy from YOU, and pay for YOUR services, because they like you and they like what you do. If you love what you are doing and you appear enthusiastic and to love what you do, then it will be much easier for customers to love you and your business.

People love enthusiasm. People love the shop assistant who knows everything about the product, and loves what she does. People love the family-run cafés and bars where the owners take such pride in what they do and how much their customers enjoy it.

Enthusiasm is infectious. If you can come over as a business owner who believes in what they are doing, and loves it, you will find the job of selling so much easier.

That love passion and enthusiasm is one of the most powerful tools for a digital marketer, and it's one of the reasons why video can be so powerful. It's much easier to project that enthusiasm when you're speaking directly to people.

Sell Yourself and Your Personality

Following on from this you must always remember that you are selling *yourself* first and foremost – not your service or product. The first step is to gain that connection and trust.

So, always try to put yourself forward with friendly enthusiasm and give generously as you can of your time and expertise.

Too many business owners think of the business itself, the name, the logo, the product or whatever as the main front for the business. This is certainly true of larger businesses where branding, expensive marketing campaigns and brand values shape an image in the minds of consumers – but the personal side is still very important.

However, a small business is not the same as a corporation. Your customers will relate to you as a person, regardless of your company's brand image. Do not hide behind names and logos and images on your website. Make sure that you, and your name, your photo and background are prominently displayed on your website, blog, videos and elsewhere. People will take much more notice of this than your logo.

People need to know who you are, and feel your motivation for what you are doing. That's where factors like image, voice and performance come in, even if you're only communicating in writing.

Loving Yourself and Your Product #2: The Power of Performance

There's no way around this. We have to talk about performance. You have to project your passion and your belief in yourself through the Social Media means at your disposal. That means written words, spoken words, photos and videos of yourself.

Some people will relish this of course. Others amongst us will feel scared to death of performing in front of a video camera. There is no need to worry about this. Skills of presentation and performance and developing your own image and voice are just that – skills. Skills can be learned and coached, and besides, remember with a video camera, or even your own phone you have all the time in the world to edit and redo. It's so much easier than doing it live!

Some of us genuinely like the sound of our own voices and don't mind at all standing up and talking in front of a crowd of people. That does not mean, of course, that the people who enjoy the performance most are actually the best at it. I am sure we have all sat at a wedding, or a conference and listened to the guy who drones on for far longer than he ought to, and tells long-winded stories with little relevance or humour.

It is a truism that the best public speakers are the ones who **practise and work** at it the most. Think of the very best speakers at a business conference or seminar or a presentation at a tradeshow. For that eloquent, effortless talk of forty-five minutes, usually you will find that at least six hours writing and practising work has gone into that performance.

So, whether or not you think you are a good public speaker, know now that you have to be prepared to do a very professional job on your performances for video, photos, written blogs or articles or even audio. There are plenty of professionals who can help with this, most of whom are not particularly expensive.

When you're starting out, however, so long as you feel the passion and the interest in what you're talking about and you believe in it, then you can do a good job with the tools you already have to hand. The video function on your phone and free video editing tools that you will already have access to, like iMovie or Windows Movie Maker can do a great job for you. In the same way, written blogs and articles usually need no more than a thorough going-over with spelling and grammar check. The best check is that you should read them aloud to see how they come over to you.

A Word about Image and Voice

It goes without saying that every human on earth projects a public image of him or herself, whether consciously or not. The world sees us in a certain way, and we have some control over that public image that we like to present.

When it comes to the public image that you're presenting through Social Media and the Internet, you have a large degree of control. The obvious aspects are taking care of your clothes, your hair and how you look in general. It is common sense that you will tailor your clothes and image to your desired audience.

However, you can go further than this and do some acting to project an image which is slightly exaggerated. In general, it is good to seem confident, friendly and knowledgeable. You could also project an image of being cocky, funny and wise-cracking. Alternatively you might want to project the image of the little guy against the corporations, or the person who is determined to bring better or cheaper services in the face of uncaring and overpriced competitors. This can be especially effective if you can focus in on a very common problem which your service or product solves.

The choice of words and the "verbal image" we create of ourselves can be very powerful.

Compare these two possible openings to a two minute video presentation about website design.

"High quality web design services can be cheaper than you think. I will take the time to understand your business, then create a website which delivers according to your business priorities, and it will likely cost you half of what you'd expect..."

"I don't know about you, but I am sick and tired of being asked to pay through the nose for website design, while dealing with techies I can't understand, and teenage designers who can't even be bothered trying to understand my business..."

Both of these approaches are completely valid. They are essentially saying the same thing, A) that this person can design and build websites for a great price, and B) that they will invest time in understanding your business. Both of these approaches are addressing perceived shortcoming in the market, ie that website design services are overpriced and a little lazy in their approach.

Now go back and read it through the two pieces once more. The first is quite plain speaking, open and honest. The second is trying to create a certain impression or personality. The second is trying to suggest that this web designer is a mould-breaker, someone who is fighting against establishment on behalf of small business people. The second approach is suggesting that this person *already understands you and your business better than his competitors do.*

In effect what the second approach has done is added a strong streak of personality or character without using any additional words or time. That persona can be witty, funny, cocky, aggrieved, passionate or whatever - using words and personality in this way can be an extremely powerful way of getting your point across and more importantly, establishing you in the mind of potential customers. It can establish you as different, unique, mould-breaking, plain-speaking and above all memorable.

All of these attributes can be desirable when you are selling yourself. This technique of establishing a certain persona by the words you use is called "voice". The voice you use should tie in with the image you wish to project, your look and any other materials you use.

The great thing about "voice" is that you can say more in the same number of words or the same 30 seconds of video. You can say: *I know you and understand your problem.*

Performance

In business, performing well usually means doing a professional job and getting it right. Makes sense? Well, that is all anyone is demanding from you in your digital marketing.

Like any other person in business, especially in marketing or selling, you are in The Attention Business.

Like it or not you have to put on a performance. That does not mean you have to be an Oscar-winning actor; it just means that you have to concentrate on doing a good job, doing it professionally and not putting it out there until you feel you have done it right.

You are in The Attention Business, and you have to perform. But then if you want to succeed in business, you always have to perform. It's nothing new.

I guess my point is that even though Social Media, YouTube or email marketing is cheap, you still have to do the very best job you can. Whatever you do, make sure you learn about techniques, get coaching if you need it, and make sure you do a good job.

Social Media marketing does not mean simply getting a few posts on Facebook and Twitter and working at it when you have a few spare minutes. It is a job of work and you have to treat it as such. You need a plan (see later).

For that matter, you may feel that keeping up a Facebook or Twitter campaign week after week and doing it well would be too time-consuming. If that's your decision then fine. Remember that you have choices and you cannot do everything or even do most of the online marketing choices before you.

The main thing is, whichever choices you make, be sure you have the time, resources and commitment to perform and to do a great job.

The really big deal about Social Media and any other digital marketing is all those figures I bombarded you with: six billion humans with access to the Internet, access to all your customers at virtually anytime via smartphone, tablet, desktop, TV and laptop, Facebook's 1.35 billion active users, YouTube's 5 billion videos each day. Those numbers are the really big deal.

The big deal is NOT that it's cheap or easy. I don't believe in the Law of Attraction, or The Law of Wishful thinking. Success comes, as ever, through hard work and applying your intelligence.

(I know it's easy to feel overwhelmed by the scale of the task, but I have some great ways of cutting through the overwhelm and simplifying everything. See later.)

Trust

Building long-term reputation and credibility = TRUST

There are huge benefits to building credibility and reputation as an expert. It's called TRUST. It's been the most sought after commodity in business since, like forever – and that's especially true in service businesses.

Think about it. If you are selling a service to a new customer, you are selling a promise. You're selling a promise that you can paint the house, or prepare someone's accounts, or repair someone's car in a competent and expert manner. That's what they pay you for. Before anyone will give you business, they have to **trust** that you can do the job. Trust is one of the oldest commodities in the world of business.

This is obvious, but TRUST is an even bigger deal in the Internet Age. Sales leads need reasons to trust that you will do what you say you will do. The Internet gives you access to vast numbers of people, but you're also one step removed from them. And you have the issue that the Internet is full of scam artists and under-deliverers. Establishing trust is even more important online. Fortunately Social Media, blogs and articles give you plenty of opportunity to establish your reputation and create that trust.

Writing blogs is good for reputation. Writing guest blogs on expert sites is better. Getting an article in the press (online or off) is great for reputation and visibility. You become and expert and an influencer and journalists begin to seek you out.

Press coverage, when you get it, is gold when it comes to reputation and credibility. It's worth thousands and often the sales are immediate. It's fantastic.

And of course the personality you can establish through your Social Media, including images and videos, can create that indefinable personal connection between you and your customer or sales lead. Social Media and online content, if done well, are an essential part of building your brand as an expert, whether as an individual or as a company.

The customers you are looking to gain are all new. You need to establish trust with them. Customers trust people, not names or logos. So make sure people know who you are and about your background.

The idea is that the customers should *like* you and *trust* you; but trust is more important.

Put it this way, it's wonderful if people like you, but in business they MUST trust you. Trust is more important than passion for your business, but then the passion and enthusiasm and the personality you project will go a long way to building that trust.

Social Media

This is also one of the reasons that Social Media can be so powerful. Personal networks created by Facebook, LinkedIn, Twitter and the rest make it 10 times easier and faster to build up the personal contact and word of mouth trust that in days gone by would have taken months and years to build up. Social Media are a bigger, faster version of word of mouth – with the advantage of pictures and video. Customer comments, reviews, recommendations, likes, tweets and testimonials are massively powerful. Social Media facilitate this creation of trust. You have to use them.

Another angle on this is to give as freely as you can of your advice and expertise – time and money permitting. People love to feel they are receiving special treatment, and they love to feel they are dealing with someone who really knows what they are talking about. It's very powerful in building trust.

Your aim with Social Media should be to make your friends and contacts and followers feel special and privileged. Of course there will be more on this later.

Be an Expert, at Being an Expert

OK, so we can all understand the benefits of being an authority and being an expert. It gives you credibility, builds trust and identifies you and your brand in the mind of potential customers.

So how do we get ourselves **recognised** as an expert and authority in our chosen area? Without that recognition you are not an expert at all! This is all about demonstrating your authority. It's all about building that credibility and then using it in such a way that you are more and more **seen** as an expert and even **invited to share** your expertise.

The Three Bs of Becoming an Expert

One guy who really has done a lot of work on this subject is Steve Scott and I shall begin with his three Bs of becoming and demonstrating that you are an expert.

1. **Be an authority**. This is particularly good if you already have a detailed understanding of your business area and years of personal experience of the work, which many others do. The idea is that you don't just talk about subject; you live and breathe the subject. You are always ready to advise, and it's obvious that you know your stuff inside out.

2. ***Borrow authority***. This is for when you have less experience, perhaps with a very niche or specific area which is nonetheless important to you. Your authority comes from knowing the people who do know all about this. You can post interviews with the expert, reference their work, or recommend some of their work. You could very well ask them to make guest blogs for instance.

This is not an admission that you are lacking in a certain area. People LOVE a web page which is a gateway to other useful pages. They will bookmark you and share your page. It's a positive.

If you think about academic papers, these people are constantly showing their authority by quoting other learning research and papers and surveys to back up what they are saying. It says that you are active in the area, and that you have done a lot of research.

Knowing the right place to look for the right information is very much a sign of authority.

3. ***Build authority***. This is where you talk about your journey all your process of acquiring knowledge and authority. You may talk about things you have tried and which did not work well. You show your passion and interest in the topic and your willingness to test things out. Most importantly, you tell stories about the breakthroughs you have made.

That's the three Bs of Authority. Let's take this further by using a practical example, and practical techniques to make you **an expert at being an expert**.

Let's take as an example Georgina, who is a therapist who uses talking therapies such as CBT and also hypnotherapy to help people who are suffering from depression, stress, anxieties and phobias.

There are *five steps* a therapist in this position can take to build up bed-rock of authority she can use to project out through Social Media, email, blogs, videos, forums and also through speaking engagements and press articles.

These five steps are dealt with in detail on my website, but they show you how to easily create authority materials and proofs which you can use on your site and then on Social Media to turbocharge your traffic.

Step 1. Case studies.

Step 2. Review books, other experts and tools.

Step 3. Define topics.

Step 4. Links to other high-quality information.

Step 5. Examples, testimonials and demonstrations.

(The guide through these five steps is a little long to include here, so I have moved it to my website www.TheAttentionBusiness.com).

Creating the right materials comes right at the centre of your Social Media campaign, as I shall explain later.

Georgina will choose which marketing methods she wants to use in order to leverage the authority material she has created. There is plenty of scope for her to share video presentations, for instance but also videos of live therapy, success testimonials and so on. The other things which play well in this space are Facebook and Twitter posts such as "five steps to beating depression", and "the link between insomnia and depression". You can use these posts to draw people into the "channel" you have created.

Later, I'll go into much more detail later about how you can leverage your authority materials using Google, Facebook, Twitter, Amazon, LinkedIn, YouTube and the other Internet Giants. For now however, you'll be able to see that acquiring all your hard-won expertise and experience is the hard part. Making your authority materials and proofs is relatively easy in comparison – and putting them out there in the right way is easier still.

Passion, Trust and Being an Expert: those are the three principles behind a strong online and Social Media presence.

So much for principles. What you need now is *a plan* so you can focus like a laser on generating squillions of traffic and leads for your business.

The Essentials of Planning for Social Media Marketing and Building Your Online Platform

There are advantages to planning your marketing, but when it comes to Social Media marketing, having a written plan and schedule is pretty much essential. It is way too easy to let your Social Media work become random, haphazard and drifting.

Not least of the reasons for planning your marketing is that if it's not written into the plan for a small business, it won't done AT ALL. A recent survey by the UK CEBR said that 73% of marketing work which small and medium enterprises had intended to do *never happened at all.*

Making a plan has the following advantages:

- Provides clear sense of direction for what you're doing
- Allocates time and resources
- Provides a basis for assessing results
- Makes someone responsible

- Stops feelings of stress and overwhelm in the face of a seemingly endless task

As I said earlier, it's not at all obvious which Social Media you should use, and then what you should be doing with them. Having a plan makes the whole thing less stressy and much less work.

Planning is the number one thing you should do to keep things easy and simple for yourself.

The made disadvantages of business planning are 1) paralysis-by-analysis and not getting on; and 2) using false assumptions. For that reason I shall keep the plan extremely simple.

Part 1. Develop a profile of your ideal target customer. This is the profile or persona at which your marketing work will be targeted. Include as much detail as you can, including market research and statistics on the demographics and background of such people. More about this later. If you have not developed this profile, you will have no idea if your content or your chosen Social Media are correct.

Part 2. Evaluate the different channels and Social Media you can choose, and make an initial choice, bearing in mind your resources. More throughout this book.

Part 3. Develop materials which will develop your brand and authority and which can be used effectively across your chosen Social Media platforms – again, this book has lots of ideas.

Part 4. Make a hierarchy of your most desired interactions (MDIs) and pick the top 3. Make sure your calls to action ease the visitors towards these MDIs.

Part 5. Having regard to your resources of time, schedule your content creation and activity. Be sure you have deadlines. Deadlines make things happen.

Part 6. Evaluate traffic and results. Make sure you do everything possible to track incoming traffic and conversions.

It's that simple. The most important aspect is the profile of your ideal customer and to bring in as much quantitative information as possible. MDIs are also extremely helpful.

A simple plan will focus your efforts like nothing else.

The Importance of Choosing Your Ideal Customer

Do you ever feel when you are looking at blogs or Facebook, or when reading some business books, that the person you are reading has created the material for himself? It's almost as if you're reading a logbook or even a diary of what that person is thinking about doing at any given moment?

Well, at the risk of saying something obvious, digital marketing, or any marketing, is not the same as this writing a diary. I know I have talked about the value of bringing yourself and your personality into Social Media marketing, but it is still critical to focus on your audience of potential customers.

Serial business entrepreneur Mike Koenig makes this point extremely forcefully. A first building block in creating any business venture is to focus on the identity, likes and dislikes and average personality of your ideal customers. What attributes to they have? How much money do they make or have to spend? What motivates them? What problems do they have that you can solve?

Koenig claims that failure to focus on the target customer is the number one reason why businesses are not successful.

When you are trying to establish your brand and reach your potential customers online, it is even easier to fail to focus on your ideal customers. They are quite removed, and for that matter it is easy to say "anyone could buy this/benefit from this". This "something for everyone" approach to marketing has never been a successful one, even for giant companies. Notice that even firms who genuinely do have something for everyone, like Amazon, focused down on a whole host of niche areas and target you ruthlessly as a customer with very finely-tuned offers.

Before starting your digital marketing campaigns, it is very useful to write out a character description of your ideal customers:

What sites do they visit online?

What they do at the weekend?

What problems do they have at work?

Their age?

Their income range?

What other products and services do they use?

What they do for fun?

What magazines do they read?

How much budget do they have to spend?

Is there business sector expanding or contracting?

What kind of margins do they make?

What annoys them?

What stresses them out?

And so on. Targeting your ideal customers with the channels you choose to get your message out there, or with the material you are using and the office you are making, is not rocket science. However you will not have a chance of succeeding if you do not do the work on profiling your ideal customer before you start.

In particular when you are putting out lots of useful information on a specific business area, it can be easier to gain followers and likes from those in the same business, and even your competitors, than to appeal to your potential customers.

This is a simple enough point, but do not neglect it. The Internet is full of brain-dumps of information, where people have just splurged out what they know about this or that topic. It's so boring.

You're in the Attention Business, and in order to grab the attention of your target customer, you have to send the right message, and you have to project the right image and persona. You have no chance of doing this unless you have a very clear written profile of your target customers.

The Inbound Marketing Revolution – What is it, and What Can It Do For You?

> An extensive study by Strata Media concluded that professional online profiling techniques, known as "Inbound Marketing", can bring in business at *63% less per sales lead* than traditional advertising and promotion. That's well below half the cost!
>
> Inbound techniques even had a one third cost advantage over "digital" techniques like Google Adwords and online banners.
>
> In truth, your business can't afford NOT to look at this as an option.

What is "Inbound Marketing"?

Modern Inbound Marketing setting up a professional and compelling presence for your business online and using it to attract business leads inwards. This means using a website, email shots, a strong presence on search engines and directories (especially Google) and on Social Media such as Facebook, LinkedIn, Twitter, Tumblr, blogs, YouTube videos and so on.

The combined effect of the online presence allows people who want your kind of product of service to find you easily and understand what's great about you.

These online media also mean it is free or low-cost to communicate with your customers and your prospects.

Your Inbound Marketing profile in effect is a gigantic Word of Mouth campaign, except that you are *steering* what is said about your business, and you are *turbocharging* that word-of-mouth, amplifying it through multiple Internet channels.

"...like turbocharging a word-of-mouth campaign, amplifying it through multiple Internet channels..."

Like much of marketing, the true aim of Inbound Marketing is not to sell, but to TELL.

Think word-of-mouth. Think tell not sell. The idea is to put the concept of your business in their minds and keep it there, through continued messages and conversation.

Inbound Marketing has some similarities with High-Probability Selling. The idea of High Probability Selling is not to waste time on hard sell with people who don't really want your product, or who can't afford it. The idea is to spend your telling time with people who want what you have and who are in the market to buy.

People aren't always ready to buy. The idea of Inbound Marketing is to establish your name in their minds for when they are ready to spend their money. It's that simple. Try and be in front of them, at "top of mind" as often as you can.

"...don't sell, TELL..."

That said – don't worry - the idea of Inbound Marketing comes with normal business expectations: **getting found, getting leads and closing sales**. One beautiful aspect of Inbound Marketing is that you can make changes to your marketing execution right now and see results today, tomorrow and next week. Instead of planning and paying for a campaign to support your latest offer, or in order to hit your end-of-month targets, you can use your Inbound Marketing set-up to make a difference at very low cost.

Basically, however, Inbound Marketing is a long term play - the longer you do it, the better the results. Marketing is a marathon, not a sprint and you need to be constantly marketing. You should never consider marketing finished. You should never "take a break." Do it every day, or at least make sure that someone is doing it for you every day.

Inbound Marketing may be cheap, but it demands *Time, Effort, Care and Attention.*

However, there are big improvements you can make **today** that will impact your results in a positive way all through the rest of the year.

On my site are 10 of the best ways to use Inbound Marketing to drive results this month:

In a nutshell, Inbound Marketing can be seen as a framework for many of the techniques we are discussing in this book. See your marketing not just as a bunch of activities that you do when you have the time. Inbound Marketing is about fitting the whole of your web presence together to drive your MDIs (Most Desired Interactions – I have a section on this later). Inbound Marketing is about establishing a solid online platform for your brand and your marketing. Usually it will centre around bringing visitors to your website, grabbing their attention when they get there, and giving them more of all the resources you have stored online for your target customers.

Your website, and your presence on the Internet in general, should be seen as the basis of your branding. It's the reputation and authority you wish to project. Your web presence is your platform for Inbound Marketing, and for your Branding.

Branding

Branding can be a slippery concept to get your arms around. In fact, for small businesses it has in the past been something of a non-issue. If an independent coffee bar, retail shop or car repair shop were to spend hours thinking about branding, you'd think they'd gone mad. For a single, independent business on the high Street, the logo combined with the personality of the owner can pretty much define the brand.

However, when we are talking about an online presence and online marketing, branding is important because it defines how you present your business to the world at large. That's not to say that branding has to be a long-winded and difficult business. You just need to take some care and bear some factors in mind.

What is Branding?

Marketers can be flaky bunch, so I will stick with the definition given by the American Marketing Association: "A brand is a customer experience represented by a collection of images and ideas; often, it refers to a symbol such as the name logo, slogan, or design scheme."

Clear? What do you mean, no??

Or: the impression of your business you wish to create in your buyer's mind.

Or: the logos, fonts, colours, images and words that represent your business and all that you stand for.

Or: Your online brand has to represent the *personality* of your business.

Now, there is a massive amount I could say about branding and its implementation online across the various Social Media, websites, emails etc. I have placed a lot more material on my website if you wish to explore this further, plan your branding and implement. There are some useful checklists and a step-by-step process you can use, and I recommend you look at them, especially to help work out your value proposition.

For now I will keep it simple and confine the dos and don'ts of branding to two elements:

Consistency

Consistency

Perhaps above all else, a successful brand online needs to be consistent. Regardless of which channel your customers see online – website, Facebook, Twitter, YouTube, blog or email – they should all have consistent and recognisable elements and tone, and they should be giving the same consistent messages.

Your online presence, regardless of the channel, should use these following elements consistently:

Tone and Voice: what would your brand sound like if it was a person? What are the words like? Professional? Sarcastic? Irreverent? Fun? Knowledgeable? Superior..? Whichever tone and voice you choose unique to stick to it across the different Social Media channels and your website.

Font: try to stick to the same fonts, and this may not be as easy as it sounds. The number of "web safe" fonts is not that huge, so check that the font you choose will render correctly on websites, iPads, phones and the rest as well as your printed material.

Colours: Choose a colour which works well online and stick with it across your media, including printed material. Make sure you get the correct Pantone name and number, and the right RGB code – and stick to them.

Design Elements: if you are using icons on your site, choose a set of consistent icons and stick to them. It is tempting to go for highly designed, complex icons, but when it comes to seeing these on mobile devices it may come unstuck. Keep it simple and keep it consistent. The same goes for use of whitespace. Keep use of whitespace consistent. If you're using photos rather than created images, again be consistent and use similar images with similar colours. Images in general are easier if you want to maintain consistency. Photos may require you to have the same actors or models for instance.

Logos: obviously logos should be the same, or you should have a consistent set of maybe three or four logos which you use.

Messaging: what are your main messages? Value? Quality? Your unique difference? Again keep this consistent across the channels.

Targeting

Your brand online should be targeted accurately at the profile and persona of your ideal customer. You will remember that working on the profile of the ideal customer is essential – especially her likes and dislikes, problems, sticking points and irritations.

Having created this ideal customer's profile you should craft your image, even your logos, colours and fonts, and your messages and offers, to appeal to that ideal customer.

This is of critical importance for online branding, since when you are online anything which is generalised, vague or unclear will go unheard. Your message should be specific, and if it is not aimed at your ideal customer, it will not be specific.

Think of a medium like Twitter. All of those millions and billions of 140 character tweets are being thrown constantly into the ether. Sometimes it seems like Twitter is a huge room full of fifty, a hundred or thousand individuals all shouting at the tops of their voices for a few seconds at a time. Who is listening? Why would anyone in that big room listen unless the message was of particular, vital interest to that individual? That's what cyberspace is like.

This is why targeting is so important to your brand. In cyberspace, no one can hear you scream – unless it was targeted specifically at them. So before you start thinking of what logos or colours or messages you are choosing to go with, think of the ideal customer and not just what appeals to you yourself.

OK, so we have talked about two elements you absolutely have to look after when it comes to branding online – consistency and targeting. There are checklists and step-by-step process lists on my website which you can use to help you develop the correct look, feel and message to put out there, and I would encourage you to at least download these and read them through.

The next thing you need to consider is how branding relates to content.

Branding = Content, Content = Branding

However carefully you have crafted your colours, fonts, images and look and feel, and however expensive or flamboyant your design has been, when it comes to your online platform, you still have to produce great, engaging, interesting content.

Boring content will create a boring brand, end of story.

So when it comes to targeting, remember to target the *content* as well as the messages and brand image.

Is the content going to grab the attention of your ideal customer?

Does the content solve this problem, or soothe that pain?

Are your customers going to use this channel at all? For instance, there is no use using Facebook for a demographic or age group which does not use Facebook.

Is the tone and voice going to appeal to your ideal customer?

Most importantly of all, are you posting on Facebook, Twitter, or a blog simply because you feel you have to?

The Joy of Digital Content – Reuse, Replay, Repurpose

Are you posting on Facebook, Twitter, or a blog simply because you feel you have to?

Now there's a question.

Look, I am very well aware that a whole lot of business owners are going to answer Yes to that question; but you can see from what we have just discussed that content needs to be targeted and consistent, and it has to be engaging to your target market. You are in The

73

Attention Business. You have to grab their attention, and then you have to keep their attention after the initial "ten second test" when they arrive at your site. After you have got them to look at your page or your post, you have approximately ten seconds to engage their interest before they click away.

So a haphazard, spur-of-the-moment approach to posting and content is never going to work.

You know what I'm going to say about content. The content you put out there should be high quality, targeted to your ideal customer, and the kind of thing they want to share. I know, I know. It all sounds like one hell of a lot of work for a small business owner who is juggling eight things at once.

And you need to do that multiple times per week across multiple platforms? Clearly that is not going to happen if you don't have a system or plan. It is almost the definition of the word "overwhelm".

The good news is that it is nowhere near that bad. As ever, the main thing you need to deal with is the "what" rather than the "how" or "how long will it take".

There are many, many quick and rapid ways to create your content. You do not need to be a writer or particularly creative. You simply need to decide what you want to say, and to know your stuff. The means to making decent and engaging content is probably in your pocket right now. If you have an Apple or Android smartphone, you will be able to record your voice for podcasts, video yourself including presentations and demos of what you do, or testimonials from your customers. Most importantly you will be able to dictate words currently into your phone and use of voice to text app to turn them straight into text you can use in blogs, forum posts or whatever.

The real joy of this comes from the reuse and re-purposing aspect of digital content. One idea, hint or set of tips and tricks, for instance, can be used as a blog post, forum post, inclusion in an e-zine, press article, read out as a podcast, the content for a video and so on. That's six pieces of content straight off, before you start re-using, linking and adapting what you have done.

The same material can also be used again for video, where it is used as a voice-over for slides, images or those hand- drawing animations you can have made for a very modest amount. Again, you probably have movie editing software already at your disposal through iMovie or Windows Movie Maker.

You still may be too busy to go ahead and create your own content in this way. However, if you decide to outsource content creation (and if you use elance.com or peopleperhour.com you can get this done very cheaply), make sure that you at least dictate an audio file of your ideas and knowledge into your phone and send it to the freelancer or content creator. The ideas have to be your OWN ideas and even if you don't get involved in the "how" of creating the content, remember that the decision about the "what" content is very much yours.

Making a professional job of your content creation is important of course. It will say a lot about your professionalism and it will be part of your brand.

Your content needs to have four main features:

Targeted - at your ideal customers.

Hook – the title or headline should book or grab the attention.

Engaging – the content should hold the attention, and be on one single topic.

Call to action – the content should naturally finish with a call to action for the potential customer.

Targeted

Let me illustrate the idea of targeting accurately with something that happened to me in the last few minutes. I have just sent out a request for quotes for some website design work. In the brief which I wrote at some length, I specified that the designer should have experience of user experience design, and preferably ideas which will appeal to teenagers in the 14 – 16 age group. I also mentioned that the programmers wanted to work with the Bootstrap responsive framework.

Thinking carefully about targeting our words now, let's look at two of the responses here.

1.

"I have 10 years' experience in designing and developing *websites.*

I have worked with Bootstrap numerous times now to develop responsive websites and it is generally my go to framework for responsive design.

I can offer a full bespoke design service to you with unlimited amendments, so you can be fully happy with the outcome. I can also code the design work I do into html 5 / css3 bootstrap responsive html templates for your developers to use to cut down on development time.

Some work I have completed in the past can be found below..."

I didn't think this was bad. It seemed like this designer knew what I was looking for, he talked about his experience, and some of the technologies I might be looking for including Bootstrap. He talked about supplying the design for developers and he mentioned responsive design, which I do want, but had failed to mention. He also said his method would save the time of the developers.

Whether I take this further will depend on the what I think of the portfolio of design work he sent me.

Contrast that with...

2.

"I hope you are well.

I am pleased to put forward my proposal for your review.

I am the sole proprietor of The Business Service. We provide website design and maintenance services, and also business services to a large number of clients across the United Kingdom.

After reading your description for this job I was very interested in your work and the project as a whole. I feel we could bring some real meaning to this new website, and help create and build a larger future for the project whilst helping the stakeholders.

Please do come back to me with any questions you may have and I will be happy to answer them for you

Many thanks

Regards

Jack"

This response shows exactly what I mean by targeting. The main problem with Jack's reply that it is way too generalized in its conception of the ideal target customer. Jack says he's the sole proprietor of The Business Service. Is it likely that he can provide all that general business advice, and also do all the technical web design work I want? Can a "sole proprietor" do all that? It's unlikely, and he's told me nothing to show that he will do the design himself, and not simply outsource it. The phrase "I feel we could bring some real meaning to this new website" is way too vague, almost meaningless.

Above all I feel that Jack is not a designer at all, but a general business adviser. He has responded to me because he can advise a little on the business aspects of web design, and, well, I suppose I am a businessman and I may need his advice.

I get the feeling that Jack would send this **exact same** proposal to any person in business, regardless of what they were looking for. The thing is, Jack may be a very useful adviser to small businesses, and offer extremely good value. But this approach to marketing simply won't work. It's too general, it's too vague and it doesn't deal with my problem or what I said I want.

The basic problem is that Jack has not identified his ideal customer, or profiled their difficulties, needs and wants. This has led to poor targeting.

So, when you are creating your content be sure it addresses the needs, wants, questions, difficulties and hot buttons of your ideal customers.

Hook Them In

|It is stating the obvious to say that there is no point in making interesting and engaging content for your platforms if you can't get people to click and look at that content in the first place.

This usually means a good headline, title or word or phrase that is certain to attract your target customers to click. It needs a *hook.*

A hook can be different for whatever line of business your end, but to fix the idea in your mind try to think of the following two concepts:

Clickbait

Heroin content

Clickbait is a word which refers to a headline or link which tempts the reader to click and take a look.

"Restaurants: eight ways to increase sales this month"

"Five steps to starting a successful food truck business"

"Teenagers should sleep more and study less"

"Lose weight on steak and beer"

Clickbait should be short, snappy phrases that grab the attention by being surprising, arresting, controversial or amazing. They can be titillating or hilarious depending on the business you are in, but merely interesting probably won't cut it. Surprising is the main thing you're looking for.

Alternatively, clickbait hooks should address exactly the current problems, stresses and strains of the target customer. That's why the "increase your sales this month" line can be so effective, because it addresses a business manager who is looking at his sales and targets for the month and wondering what on earth he or she can do in the very short term to pull this around. You would have to have a genuine solution to that problem, however.

Heroin Content – Careful with This

Heroin content is something like a Holy Grail of Internet marketing. It refers to secrets, pictures or whatever else that everyone wants to see, or a solution to a seemingly impossible problem.

Genuine heroin content or products are extremely rare of course. Most of the heroin content-type headlines that you see on the Internet are the gateway to some kind of deception or scam. Secrets or products that make men irresistible to women, or make their penises bigger, or allow women to lose weight effortlessly, or get rich quick schemes are obvious examples.

I mention this heroin content not because I am encouraging you to use this tactic, but because even if you do have a superb product which will solve a very difficult problem, you do not want to be associated with the scammers and spammers out there. Accordingly, you need to be sensitive in how you pitch this to your ideal customers, and you need plenty of background and believable proofs.

Engaging

This is kind of obvious, but the content needs to be engaging, and in a format that will engage your target market. Remember, huge swathes of society do not like to read too much. Only 35% of consumers ever visit a bookstore, and that was the case even before Amazon came along. People do not like to read too much.

So think about the demographic and the educational background of your target customers and ask yourself if it will be better getting your point across in a short video.

Remember, boring content = boring brand. And, regardless of how much work you have put into a piece of content, if you reread it and think it is boring, either scrap it or change it radically. There is no other way.

Calls to Action

All your content should naturally finish up with a call to action, either to click on a link to know more, signup to a mailing list, make a phone call or request a phone call. This means that you should by no means be telling everything and giving everything away in the content you put out there. You need to give them a reason to take the next step and make a further interaction.

For this reason your content should be crafted in a way that it leaves them wanting to know more! At least a little more…

Later on I shall be talking about MDIs, or Most Desired Interactions. You should definitely read that before you think about what your calls to action will be.

But right about now in the book, I'm guessing you're feeling overwhelmed about the scale of the work you're signing up to. Don't worry. In the next chapter we're going to cut right through and deal with the overwhelm problem…

HELP! OVERWHELM! "I Don't Have Time for All This Stuff!" The

Simple Way to Deal with Overwhelm and Get On with Marketing...

As I said at the beginning of this book, I have been down this road myself. I have progressively, down the years, tried to keep ahead of techniques in online marketing and to use whatever tools were available to me. That was OK when we were restricted to banner ads, building some community websites and email marketing.

However, right now it is impossible to know it all and know the tips and tricks in enough detail. What's more, without a team of half a dozen marketing staff, it would be impossible to do it all.

This chapter is about cutting through the overwhelm and getting on with some marketing. For small businesses, procrastination and not knowing where to start are the main problems. A UK survey done by the highly respected CEBR revealed that, of the small amount of marketing planned by small and medium businesses in 2013, only 40% was carried out. If we take this to small businesses of fewer than nine staff, it's worse. The vast majority of the marketing work they intend to do never gets done.

There are *six quick techniques* which can quickly deal with the problem of overwhelm and allow you to get on with marketing and running your business. Build these techniques into your written marketing plan.

Targeting

I won't repeat myself here but creating the most detailed profile you can of your ideal customer, with their likes, dislikes, problems, annoyances, sticking points and likely budget is critical.

Only when you have profiled your ideal customer can you look at your own offering and see how your value proposition meets their needs and wants. This targeting need not take a long time, and if you're already in business you will know a great deal about your customers and you should be able to jot down these details quite quickly.

Again, if you don't like writing, just make yourself a voice memo on your phone, and if you want, get it turned to written notes by using a voice-to-text app. If you have iPhone 5 or later, the built-in voice to text function is excellent; if you have android or iPhone 4 you can download an app such as Dragon to do this for you and it works very well.

Choosing the "What" and not the "How"

It is tempting with Social Media marketing to get on and mend the activities you have already been doing, perhaps half-heartedly. You may have used Twitter or Facebook to no great effect, and you want to know how to use these two giant platforms more effectively.

STOP! If you do this you will find there is a never ending amount of information on how to use Facebook alone. There is page after page out there, article after article, and that's just for one Social Media platform!

You must not do it that way. Go through your targeting process and work out your value proposition to your ideal customer. Then go through the notes in this book and work out which platforms are going to be most effective for you. Work out which content you need and make a proper plan.

The most important way of dealing with overwhelm is to focus, focus and focus again. You have focused on your ideal customer, focused on your value proposition to the customer, and what you want to say. Now you need to choose on which marketing method is going to work best and focus on that.

It may be that you only have time and resources for one or two online platforms. That's fine. You need to focus on each one and make sure you do it professionally and well.

(However, if you put targeted content at the centre of your plan, you'll see that it's easy to hit six or seven Social Media platforms).

What you must NOT do is spend days reading about Facebook tips, techniques and advertising, and then realise you should be concentrating on Google search optimization, or LinkedIn for instance.

When you have decided "what" you need to do, then the Zulu Principle comes into play.

The Zulu Principle

The Zulu Principle is a phrase coined by a stock analyst and fund manager called Jim Slater in the 1970s.

It's a memorable phrase and Slater tells the story of how he came up with it. He said he was watching TV one night with his wife, and there was some mention or short piece about the Zulus in South Africa. His wife made some comment, Jim Slater asked her why she had said that, and over the next ten or fifteen minutes she explained to him all about Zulu history, culture and society, and was able to answer any question he could dream up.

Slater asked his wife how and why she had come by all this knowledge about the Zulus. The answer is quite simple and obvious. Mrs Slater had seen a documentary about the Zulus, and it had piqued her interest. She went on to watch any other television shows about Zulus, and go to the library to find books about Zulu history.

Slater's point was that you can't know everything, you can't be an expert across the board; but you can be an expert on any one thing, so long as it is a specific niche subject. The point of the Zulu Principle for investment management was that if you stick to one business sector and do your research and know everything about it, you can be very successful. Conversely, if you try to know a bit of everything you are asking to fail.

The Zulu Principle is a very valuable idea across all of business. Working in niches, focusing and being an expert in a particular is proven time and time again to be more profitable than trying to offer something for everyone.

Do not try to master Social Media across-the-board. Try to focus on one or two of the most effective platforms, and if you have people working for you, you can get another person to focus on another area in the same way.

Or, you can use a small amount of money and get someone else to do your focusing for you. You can outsource some or all of your Social Media marketing.

Don't let yourself get captured by the complexity of all the different channels. Choose which ones you can exploit, then either focus on each in turn or outsource as needed.

MDI's

Ranking your Most Desired Interactions and focusing on the top three will help enormously to focus your activity. See the chapter on Most Desired Interactions.

Outsourcing

Outsourcing will cost you money of course, but there are a number of very good reasons why you should outsource this rather than doing it yourself. The main reason of course is that you should be working on your business and not spending hours working with Social Media.

Certain Social Media platforms, such as Facebook, blogging and Twitter can be very time-consuming. Again if you use elance.com or peopleperhour.com, you will easily find people to do the work cheaply and effectively. Make sure you give them a small amount of work to try them out at first.

The most important thing about outsourcing this marketing work is that the decision comes after YOU have done the targeting and profiling work and after

YOU have decided what marketing work needs doing. Outsource the "how", and never the "what". You can do this together with a marketing professional to advise you if you like, but remember this is your business and these are critical decisions. It's like making a major decision about choosing a supplier. You might consult, you might take advice, but in the end it's your decision.

Focus on targeting your offer to your ideal customers, and then decide what marketing channels are going to be best. That is the "what". The "how" is how you market effectively with your chosen online channels.

When you are choosing how to do the work, you either follow the Zulu Principle and focus on one technique at a time in detail, or you outsource.

Dealing with the overwhelm is that simple.

Time-Saving Tools

Another must have is software tools to automate and speed your social media work. There are some excellent choices out there, and although you'll pay to use the best ones, others are free. I highly recommend these tools. Mostly they are there to automate the posting of blogs, vlogs and video to a wide range of sites and Social Networks, and to make sure you do a really great job of that repetitive task.

These tools can bring huge traffic to your site or Social Media and they allow you to focus on content creation. You'd be mad not to use them.

See a review of the tools at:

www.TheAttentionBusiness.com

PART TWO

CHOOSING YOUR ONLINE PLATFORMS AND MAKING THE MOST OF THEM

HOW TO CHOOSE WHICH SOCIAL MEDIA

(Although the average "Social Media Professional" uses seven different Social Media channels, you may not have time for that many. However, remember that by <u>putting content at the heart of your campaign, and by</u> <u>using automation tools</u>, it's relatively easy to work across a number of channels without suffering overwhelm.)

Remember that I said choosing which marketing channels to use is like choosing a major supplier? Well that's true if you think about.

Imagine for a moment that you had a bicycle shop, and you were also branching out to selling bikes, parts and accessories on a website. You will have to choose your suppliers with care and due diligence to make sure the quality, price and delivery are right.

If the prices from your supplier for the bikes and the components are too high, your offering will not be competitive or you will not make money. If the supplier cannot deliver fast enough, you will get complaints, emails and phone calls hassling you, which cost you time, money and loss of reputation. If the quality of anything you are offering is not good enough, products will be sent back, you will generate extra work, emails and phone calls, and it will generate a bad reputation.

So the downsides of choosing a poor supplier are losing money and margin, extra time spent wastefully, and cost to your reputation. Choosing the wrong Social Media or web platform to spend your time and money on can cost you in **exactly the same way**.

Choosing to concentrate on Facebook and/or Twitter when they are not appropriate can cost you hugely in time.

Choosing to spend money on Google Adwords and Google optimization when you do not have an effective website to monetise that traffic, can become a huge waste of money.

And then losing control of the messages you are sending on Social Media and emails can cost your reputation if they are not consistent, they are promising things you cannot deliver, or simply that the tone quality of the messages is not what it should be.

So the selection of which media you can commit to is an important choice for you.

Decision Criteria

For each of the major Social Media or giant web platforms I discuss here, I will just start with a simple list of advantages and disadvantages. This means what these platforms are good for and what may be difficult about them. These simple advantages and disadvantages of each platform should be the starting point for your choices. As I have said before, each business is unique and will need a different approach. You will need to think through all possibilities carefully.

What you can't do is think: "Everyone I know is using Twitter. I need to be on Twitter."

In particular you should work out your MDIs (discussed alongside websites below) and how you could achieve them through the various platforms.

All the while remember that you need to cut through the overwhelm and FOCUS on one channel at a time, or pay money to outsource it.

We start our review of the online channels with your website, and what you want it to do for your business.

Your Website and What it Should Be

Last year, I listened to a speech by a well-known US marketing expert who has been extremely successful in her businesses. The first thing she said was this:

"If you take away one thing today, it should be that whatever business you are in, you need a really good website. Just having any website is not good enough, it needs to be the best it can be."

Well, that sounds true, doesn't it? It might not be easy, given the high standard of websites out there, but her statement does sound absolutely right.

The fact is, for most people and businesses, that statement IS correct. Mostly, there is no point marketing, networking, giving out business cards, sending mailshots or any of it unless you have a wonderfully professional web presence to send your potential customers to. If you give someone a business card, and she is interested in what you spoke about, the first thing she will do is to look at your site; and she will judge you on that site. It's that simple. Most businesses will need the best web presence they can manage.

However, before we go further I should say that it is not *essential* to have a website at all. Take for example the clock lady called Sue who I mentioned earlier. Her main business is all through Amazon in the UK, and then she markets through Amazon in the US, and now Australia. She does not have a website, and in truth she does not need one. Amazon provides her an excellent online platform and if she had website it would only be stepping stone to the Amazon ordering page in any case. For Sue, having a website would actually **divert** customers away from her main web presence, which is on Amazon.

The same could be said for eBay traders.

The important thing is that you need an excellent web presence or platform. You can choose to have a website, and most of us do, but you can use one of the other options to establish your web presence. Wherever you choose to have your main web presence, you must make it as good as you can, and maintain it.

For Sue, the great thing about having her presence on Amazon is that she wants the site to do two things: showcase her product and sell efficiently. Amazon is excellent for that, and completely focused. For Sue it is a great choice.

It would not be the same for everyone.

Websites: The Swiss Army Knife Factor

The good thing about websites is that they are almost infinitely flexible. They can do so many things for you. Websites can give out information, they can show videos, they can distribute podcasts, a can sell things by e-commerce, they can act as a library of information for your customers, they can host forums, blogs, interactive chat, they can act as your product database, they can host webinars, they can make giveaways, collect details and so on and so on.

Not only can websites do all these things for you, they can usually do them more quickly, saving you money, man-hours and resources. Websites work 24/7, and once you have set them up they are a very low cost way of providing services.

So you can see why I call websites the Swiss Army Knives of business and marketing. They are like a multitool; they can do so many things for you.

That *flexibility* is a good point and the bad point of websites. It is so easy to lose focus on what your website should be doing for you. Remember: this book is about **choices and focus** – cutting through the overwhelm by making the right choices and applying focus.

I have advised and project-managed so many website builds for small and medium businesses, and it is so easy to look around at competition or other websites and say "look, that feature is cool; look - that widget would look good on our site". Yes, features and functionality are good, but for small and medium businesses you need to focus your web visitors to do what you want them to do.

The way to make the right choices of what your website should be doing for you, and focus correctly is by using MDIs – Most Desired Interactions. I shall discuss these very shortly, but first let's have a look at some of the essentials you need to have top-of-mind if you are building a website today.

Essentials of Business Website Functionality

Website Essential #1: Build Assets

This is the most important mindset about your website. In fact, building <u>business assets</u> goes through to the whole philosophy of a business model. Think of your website as creating long-term value. Your website is your storefront, your store interior, all of your marketing materials and your personality in fact. *It's your brand.*

I said just above that you are not forced to have a website, so long as you have another highly effective website presence. The good thing about having a website, however, is that it is yours and totally under your control. You are not at the mercy of changes in Facebook rules, changes in the Google algorithm, search results on YouTube, Amazon's system, or anything else. A website is yours, it's a long-term asset and you should use it to create long-term assets in your business.

In this case, long-term assets in your business mean long-term, profitable customer relationships. So, by "building assets" I mean you want these kind of interactions on your website:

Joining your email list

Giving further data about themselves

Building a relationship through interactions on your website

Sharing your content

Bringing others to your site

Downloading information

Enjoying and recommending your videos and podcasts

Picking up the phone to you

Buying products or services

Contributing to your blog or forum

Asking questions

Leaving comments or reviews (positive reviews are gold)

Social Media likes, pins, tweets, recommends and shares of all kinds

Long-term relationships (assets) are built by interactions on your website, and the deeper and more committed those interactions are, the more valuable they are to your business. They mean a deeper relationship with a customer which adds to your brand, your authority and the size of your lists.

Sure, you want to sell things and make money now, but it's a whole lot easier if you have an email list, or a long list of Twitter followers or Facebook friends. Building up these Social Media list-assets gives you power in the future.

When you see a list of interactions like the one above, you are back with the problem of overwhelm. *"Can I really encourage all these interactions? Which should I focus on?"* We manage this problem by analysing Most Desired Interactions and focusing on the top three in order of importance. More later.

Website Essential #2: Mobile

Going mobile is the second essential of a website in 2014. You have to go mobile-enabled and responsive. There is no sense building a website that isn't.

There are **way** more tablets and smart phones out there than there are laptops and desktops, and they are used **way** more often. Already, 78% of Facebook's pageviews are on smartphones. That can be a scary figure if you have an old-fashioned website – even one a couple of years old!

It used to be expensive to get a website that functioned well on a smartphone, but that is no longer true. Up until a year or so ago, designers would actually create two whole sites if you wanted to be mobile friendly! They would build the site and then another site that worked well on mobile. Imagine maintaining both those websites at once!

Now you can get your developer to use a responsive framework to build your site; or if you're doing things yourself, you can choose one of the responsive frameworks on WordPress for instance. **You must insist on this.**

Website Essential #3: Simplicity, and Simple Navigation

The French writer, Antoine de Saint Exupery, said that perfection was achieved not when everything had been added, but when everything unnecessary had been taken away.

In the same way, your website should be free of unnecessary distractions, and by that I mean distractions from your three main MDIs. Don't clutter your website real estate with unnecessary background information. You can have an information-packed site, but items, articles and links which are background should be treated as such and put into your sidebars or even in the footer.

Remember to put your most important calls to action high on the right-hand side. Eye-tracking studies have shown that this area is by far the favourite resting place for eyeballs in the first ten seconds of viewing the page. That is why Amazon placed their buy button in that top right position, and if you have a Google Toolbar that is where the Google search box resides.

Clearly, there are some big, successful websites out there with plenty of clutter on the page. Amazon is an obvious example, but if you look at the homepage, or *your* Amazon homepage, since it is customised to you as a user, it is simple and single-minded in its purpose.

So visitors should find what they want easily and without getting confused. More importantly, your visitors should find **what you want them to find** and what you want them to do online. Again this comes down to your Most Desired Interactions. Once you are clear what you want visitors to do in your site, design issues very easily sort themselves out.

All this sounds very common sense and obvious. However, remember that the reason why most websites, especially smaller websites, become confusing and sometimes difficult to navigate is that the website owner has given a list of pages and desired functions to the website designer. The website designer usually has her own priorities around doing the work quickly and easily. Very often the designer will choose to use a framework she has used before, and will simply fit your content and the functions you wanted on top of that framework. Not surprisingly, this can result in confusing results, since ***you have effectively got your own content fitted on top of someone else's navigation logic.***

This is especially true of e-commerce sites, generic job boards and other functional sites which are based on commonly available templates. The templates were designed for someone else, and they are also designed to cover every possible eventuality. The result is that a designer will come up with forms which demand far too much information, throw up pointless error messages and are confusing to use.

Over the last five years, how often have you been on website after it has been revamped and asked yourself why it is more difficult to use than the old one? This has arisen as website creation tools have become more and more complex. Designers have used clever-looking templates and retro-fitted the site onto them!

Remember - you are the owner of the site, and you should demand that it works smoothly and keeps it simple for your customers!

Start with a wish list of elements and functionality of the site and cross out ruthlessly everything that is unnecessary, **may** be useful or "nice to have". At first, keep the site to the bare bones of your desired interactions. The time to add functionality and features is after the site has been running and you have done surveys of users to see which functions or features they would like added or changed.

When you are envisaging how the site should look, start with how you imagine it should look on a smartphone. If you start from that point, and focus ruthlessly on your MDIs, then the simplicity of use and usability should flow well from that point. You can't put too much clutter on a phone screen.

OK, let's move on now to MDIs, since they are critical to the design of your website, and your choice of Social Media, and in fact critical to your whole business model.

Most Desired Interactions – MDIs

Working out your Most Desired Interactions for your online presence is one of the best things you can do to make choices, focus on what's important, and generally de-clutter your planning for marketing. It helps you focus once again on the "what" rather than the "how", and it helps you cut through the issue of overwhelm when faced with all the tasks around online and Social Media marketing.

I have referred to MDIs quite a bit along the way, especially in the section on websites; but they are relevant to other Social Media such as Facebook and Twitter.

Thinking back to our website planning, we can make a list of positive interactions we might get from visitors to our site, bearing in mind that we want a profitable long-term relationship with the visitor.

Joining your email list

Giving further data about themselves

Building a relationship through interactions on your website

Sharing your content

Bringing others to your site

Downloading information

Enjoying and recommending your videos and podcasts

106

Picking up the phone to you

Buying products or services

Contributing to your blog or forum

Asking questions

Leaving comments or reviews (positive reviews are gold)

Sharing your content on Facebook or Twitter

Generally wanting to know more

I mentioned before that the main point of MDIs is to help you choose what to do on your website or Social Media, and to focus down on your priorities. You need to look at your business model and rank these interactions 1,2,3 etc. Remember, they are ALL desirable, but you have to choose the top three.

The MDI work acts as a *decision hierarchy*. You want a new visitor to do the first action, but if she doesn't, then you provide an alternative that's *still* mutually beneficial.

So if your goal is sell products by ecommerce, then your MDIs could be:

1. Subscribe to an email list
2. Buy products
3. Leave reviews on products

Or let's say you're a restaurant owner, then your website MDIs might be:

1. Subscribe to an email list
2. Make a restaurant booking
3. Share it on Social Media

Finally, let's say you're a service business, like a tax accountant, then your MDIs will be:

1. Subscribe to an email list
2. Buy a service or request a call
3. Share downloaded information with others

The MDIs might be different in your opinion of course, and remember they're _all_ desirable, but you have to choose three. This will help focus you in your choices and it will help the visitor interact with you. If you give your visitor too much choice, it tends to dissipate the experience, to the point where that person just decides to come back "when they have some time". That's not so bad, but it's not what you want, and you should concentrate on getting his email address.

Notice how the first MDI is **always** "subscribe to an email list." A good email list from your target market can be your biggest asset in marketing, and sometimes in your whole business. Always look for email subscribers.

The Attention Business in the age of Internet marketing is always going to suffer from the problem of _overwhelm_, and that problem is only going to get worse. Overwhelm may be your biggest problem in fact.

Simple analysis tricks like the Ideal Customer Profile and the Most Desired Interactions, that needn't take more than a few minutes, will help you focus like a laser beam on where to place your efforts.

The other thing about the MDIs is, well, they're the whole point! Without some key interactions in mind, all this Attention Business is just so much activity. The point of the Attention Business is in the name. It is a business. It's easy to see that with a website – you spent money on it and it has to work for your business. But with Social Media? Well, that's free isn't it? It's so easy to get drawn into essentially pointless activity with Social Media, posting on Twitter and Facebook with no MDIs in mind at all.

Don't do pointless stuff. Make your choices, focus, and have a plan.

So much for interactions. The next two chapters are all about content which you can use to draw your ideal customers to your site and make those interactions. Next up are blogging and then videos.

Blogging, White Papers and Articles to Download

Advantages:

- Draws Google traffic

- Builds authority and image as an expert
- Builds your brand
- Makes your site "sticky"
- Makes your site shareable
- Gives you material for high quality posts on Twitter, LinkedIn, Facebook etc
- Low cost in money
- Material can be re-used, split up or collected together as articles, e-zines, newsletter, press releases, ebooks, white papers, videos, podcasts and webinars
- Can be used with "permission-gating" to gather email addresses
- ***Creating shareable content like this is at the centre of your Social Media campaign.***

Disadvantages:

- Time-consuming

Must-do factors

- Do quantitative keyword and niche topic research to confirm your content is on target
- Use this content to steer visitors towards your MDIs

Obviously, creating blogs, articles and white papers is time-consuming. So is making videos, podcasts and infographics to share.

So why a small business person would do this – or pay for it to be done? Let me tell you that as of 2014,

63% of marketers in B2B businesses in the US use content creation marketing, so there *is* a point to it. Larger firms appoint a dedicated person or even a team to do this work. Why?

The simple reason is that high quality, targeted content attracts high quality, targeted sales leads and visitors. Which is what we all want.

High quality, targeted content can also be used time and time again to enhance your Social Media posts on LinkedIn, Facebook, Twitter, YouTube, Google+ and more to give you authority. It makes your Social Media work a hundred times easier.

In fact, Social Media Examiner website says *"it goes without saying that your blog should be at the center of your Social Media marketing activity"*. Basically, content from your blogs, articles, videos and so on comes first, and then the other Social Media posts refer to that content and use that content. That's how it works.

INFOGRAPHIC ON THE IDEAS FACTORY - CONTENT AT THE CENTRE OF SOCIAL MEDIA PROCESS

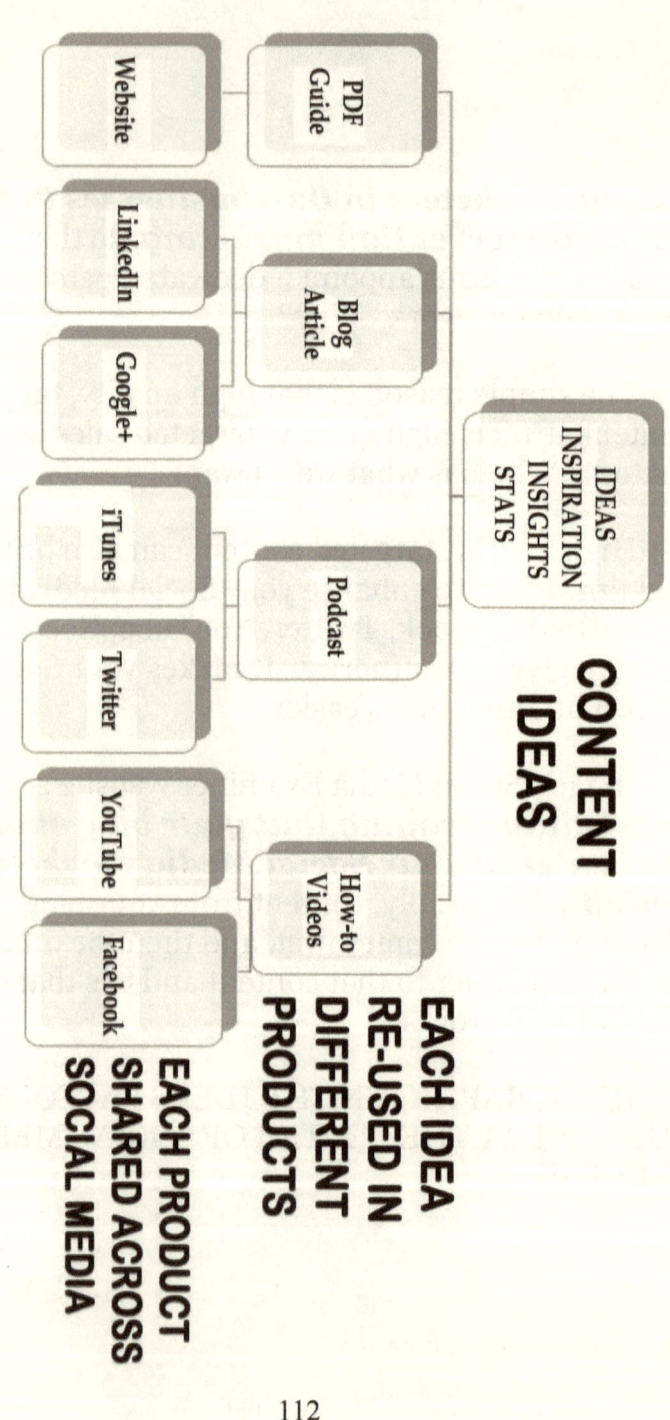

CONTENT IDEAS

IDEAS
INSPIRATION
INSIGHTS
STATS

PDF
Guide

Website

Blog
Article

LinkedIn

Google+

Podcast

iTunes

Twitter

How-to
Videos

YouTube

Facebook

EACH IDEA
RE-USED IN
DIFFERENT
PRODUCTS

EACH PRODUCT
SHARED ACROSS
SOCIAL MEDIA

Far from being a time-consuming, peripheral activity, creating blogs, videos and content can be the most effective way of marketing across a number of Social Media channels.

One idea can spawn three or maybe four products – a blog, a video, an infographic and a podcast. There is room for articles in e-zines, white papers and who knows what else besides, but let's just say there are four.

Those four products can then posted across say six or eight Social media as well as your website. Immediately you have twenty-four high quality posts from the same idea, and let's be honest, if you're using some of the automated posting tools out there, it could be a whole lot more than that!

If you plan this content creation process in at the start, the rest of your Social Media activity schedule pretty much falls into place around it. It's much less work!!

Content creation simplifies and clarifies the process.

Content creation lets you mobilize multiple social platforms effortlessly

Content creation keeps the eyeballs on you, rather than directing them away to someone else's content!

Let's go through the must dos and then the advantages of content and blogging in a little more detail.

Content Must-dos

Make sure your content is data-driven.

Matthew Capala writes "if you engage in content marketing and you don't have ideal customer profiles developed and validated by quantitative research, start over." By personas, Matthew means.

Creating blogs and content is time-consuming, right? So the content you create had better work for you out of the blocks. No one wants to "start over".

Go back to your ideal customer profiles, work on topics and keyword targeting which will attract and engage your ideal customers, and then make sure you use some of the keyword and niche testing tools out there to validate your choice of topics and the words you are using, especially your subject headers, and HTML page titles.

This kind of quantitative work for selecting topics and keywords is not that difficult, but I have a short guide to the most useful keyword analysis tools on my website:

www.TheAttentionBusiness.com

Engage with the search engine optimization issues before you start. Again content creation is time-consuming, so you want to get it right first time.

The best time to engage with SEO is while you're still conceiving and building your website. This may not be possible of course, but you should certainly focus on SEO issues when you start creating your blog. It even affects the platform or content management system you choose and the structure of your blog site.

One of the advantages of starting a blog on WordPress, for instance, is that it has so many search engine-friendly features built in, and it naturally attracts Google traffic from day one. I would recommend making it easy for yourself. You do not need to re-invent the wheel. WordPress is designed for blogging and information websites and it can be very powerful if you utilise all its features.

Until about a year ago, there was a bad tendency for blogs and online articles to be so densely covered with keywords in bold or italics, that they were just about unreadable. The Panda change to the Google algorithm in 2013 has changed how you should approach things. Thankfully Google has downgraded sites which use this "keyword spamming" and values high quality, engaging content more highly. It also measures the level of engagement by how often the blogs or articles are shared on Social Media. Therefore the rule of thumb is to think of your ideal customers first to hook and engage them; and think of the Google algorithm second.

Pull your visitors towards your MDIs. So, great content is targeted to pre-defined customer profiles, and optimised to search engines. If you have achieved that your material will naturally pull in your desired audience, so you don't need to be too pushy about moving them towards your most desired interactions. They will tend to want to do your MDIs, for instance they will be interested in your report or ebook and be happy to give their email address in order to gain access to it.

However, while you do not want to be too pushy, you want to limit choice and drive a user through your content towards your MDIs and your calls to action.

Most of the list of advantages I have given for blogs and content creation are self-explanatory, but I can explain a couple of points on the different advantages:

- *Draws Google traffic* - see comments on search engine optimization above.
- *Builds authority and image as an expert* - it is important to give of your knowledge. Content marketing is definitely a case of "give to receive" situation. If you're giving useful information, especially in a conversational but professional tone, it will go down well and you will be engaging. There should be *value* in what you are putting out there for your ideal customers.
- *Builds your brand* - building authority and your persona as an expert of course adds to your brand. It gives depth and background and personality to your brand, in a way that logos, slogans and one-liners cannot.
- *Makes your site "sticky"* - of course you want online visitors to stay around and to come back. You also want them to share your material with others in their network.
- *Makes your site "shareable"* – which gets you seen and boosts your Google ranking.

- *Gives you material for high quality posts on Twitter, LinkedIn, Facebook etc* - you can use your blog posts and articles to draw in visitors from all over your Social Media channels. There will be other campaigns you wish to run on Facebook, Twitter or LinkedIn, but your blog is central to much of it. High quality content allows you to work across five or six Social Media channels at once, rather than working on posts for one at a time.
- *Low-cost in money*
- *Material can be re-used, split up or collected together as articles, ezines, newsletter, press releases, ebooks, white papers, videos, podcasts and webinars* - not only can your content be used across different Social Media channels, it can be used to post on other sites, YouTube, repurposed etc ALL of this brings traffic back to you.
- *Can be used with "permission-gating" to gather email addresses* - permission gating is where you allow access to a report, e-book or other information product when the visitor provides her email address. It's a very common practice, and you will know yourself that you are only likely to give that permission these days if you are genuinely interested in the information product, and if you think it is going to be worth it to give your email address. So, in order not to disappoint your visitors, and ruin the whole effect, make sure the information products you use for

permission-gating are genuinely useful and valuable, and that you do not mis-use the email addresses.

Google Optimization

Advantages:

- Free
- Effects last long-term
- Brings you the power of Google, which is unrivalled
- Long-tail searches can bring you exactly the people who are searching for your offering

Disadvantages:

- Getting search optimization right is difficult and you are always at the mercy of changes in Google's rules and systems
- Although you can make an effort to make this work, so can everyone else! It's extremely difficult for popular topics
- It can be powerful but unreliable. The best piece of advice is "build your website optimised for Google, but build your business as if Google could disappear tomorrow".

The main factors for success with search optimization are always subject to the changes and the vicissitudes of Google, but basically they come down to 3 factors: site design, relevancy and linking and embedding. To this can be added – how often shared on Social Media.

I myself have written hundreds of pages on these three topics, and I do not intend to try and give a full account of it all here. Especially when it comes to site design, file types, filenames and web server technologies, you're going to have to use an expert anyway.

As ever, much more is available at my website, www.theattentionbusiness.com, and I will limit myself to some must-do comments.

Optimization Must-do #1: Site design – if you are at the stage of having a site built, ask the questions about search engine optimization at this stage. To be honest, most web designers and developers are well on top of this topic, but beware of designers who like image-heavy homepages with Flash animations. In days gone by, some site architectures would not have shown up on Google at all. That's no longer the case, but some pages, especially static HTML pages, work much better than others.

Also, build your keywords into the page title tag, the content tag, and the URL. Web professionals will help you with this.

Optimization Must-do #2: Relevancy – this is all about how relevant your content is to any given search. As I said before, use the keyword tools I have pointed you towards, and make sure the keywords are aimed well at your ideal customer profile. That is the starting point for relevancy. Simple enough. Don't use popular keywords if they don't work for your target audience.

Much greater weight is given to keywords if they are included in the title URL, page title or in page headers. There is also greater weight given if the keywords are included in hyperlinks, and if the keywords are also included in the pages you are linking to. In other words, not only should your keywords be relevant, but your outbound and inbound links should also be relevant to your target searchers.

Bear in mind that it is extremely difficult to target searchers of one or two words. It's just too broad. Try and home-in more with searches of three or four words or even five words. These days, Google searchers are savvier and much more likely to use a more finely tuned search term. In fact, you will notice that Google is constantly filling in suggested search terms for you as you type into the search box. So where your searchers may have started with the intention to search on two words they will very often be guided to search on a three or four words string.

Try putting your two word search terms into the Google search box and see what suggestions it makes, because these will be ranked in order of likelihood. If you can optimize your material to the top couple of searches, you are going to do well.

Optimization Must-do #3: Long-tail relevancy – this is a term given to the millions of exact, very specific search terms which are used all the time on Google. It may be that each search term is not common at all, but because searchers use these specific, exact search terms over time in their millions, these long-tail searches make up over 50% of the searches on Google.

Not only that, but long-tail search terms have two big advantages. Firstly, because the searches are relatively uncommon, it is much easier to rank highly in the first page of Google for these searches. Secondly these specific, exact search terms are likely to bring the visitors who are precisely interested in what you are offering, so there is no waste. If you can get well ranked in Google.

An example of this is product titles or product reference numbers. If you can use the exact product title, manufacturer and their product reference number in your HTML page title, URL and in the header on the page you have a very good chance of ranking in Google for those searches. Searchers online are often looking for very specific things, so you should build separate pages to respond to those exact products, and not simply use your own product or page numbers.

The other issue with relevancy is that frequency is an issue. If your webpages are static and do not change, they will tend to be downgraded by Google. The more often your site and pages are updated with new, relevant and engaging information, the better your rankings will be.

IMPORTANT POINT – It is too easy to start using keyword research tools to see how often certain words and phrases come up in search terms on Google. You can be mesmerized by how many visitors are available. Your focus however should always be on your ideal customer profile. The important thing is not what was typed in the search box, *but who typed it*. Do not water down what you are aiming at. After all, Google itself is completing millions of search terms before users have even finished typing! This means that the terms which appear to be popular will just become more popular. Always put your ideal customer profile first.

That is a very simple description of the issue, and for many readers that will be a drastic oversimplification. For that I apologise. Again please look at my site, www.TheAttentionBusiness.com where there is much more information on this topic.

The real action for search optimization in Google and Social Media is with linking and popularity.

Linking, embedding and popularity - Google's system has long allocated a rating, Pagerank to each website and web page. The higher your page rank on a scale of one to 10, the more likely you are to come high on the Google search results. Only a couple of sites in the world are accorded page rank ten, including Google itself and the download page for Adobe Reader, which is linked to by millions of pages across the web. At the other end of the scale page rank one is virtually an unknown, unvisited site.

In the middle of the scale, page rank three is quite decent, and page rank seven is a very considerable achievement. If you get to page rank five or six you can congratulate yourself.

The way the system works is that Google looks at the popularity of your site in terms of the number of page views and traffic. It also looks at the links from your site going outwards, and back links from other sites going to your pages. However, links from other sites which are low in page rank have very little effect on your standing. What you are looking for is links from big, well known sites with high reputation and authority, such as government sites, news sites and so on. Links from these sites will also increase your traffic of course.

Link building used to be a long-term, constant labour of the website owner. However, this is where use of Social Media really works. By posting references and links to your blogs and content across Social Media, you gain incoming links and your network is able to share these links, multiplying them across the networks of Social Media. If one of your posts proves popular it will boost your page rank and your Google positioning as well as simply bringing you traffic in the short term.

Shareable content creates long-term value in search engine optimization and your site's ranking.

In this way, high-quality, relevant content, backed up with posts and sharing across Social Media can have not only a short-term effect on your traffic, but a long-term effect from boosting you on Google.

Remember also that Google likes websites where the relevant, engaging material is updated very regularly. Blogs are the perfect way of doing this.

This is an almost embarrassingly concise description of the value of search engine optimization, but I hope you can see the main point. Search engine optimization is a speciality, but it ties in very closely with blogs, content creation and frequent posting on the Social Media. All of these factors work together to boost each other, build your brand and increase your traffic.

Hopefully you are beginning to see how the whole integrated system works together.

Next up is video, and the YouTube platform.

Video – YouTube, Vimeo, DailyMotion and More

Advantages:

- For most of the population, video is more engaging than text
- YouTube has more searches than any other platform
- For a younger demographic it is THE source of information
- Concise and easy to get your point across
- Videos are easy to make and don't take much time to produce
- Immediate, punchy, memorable and shareable

- Videos rank high on Google
- You can use a strong call to action
- You can create mood and brand associations with music and arresting footage and images
- Your personality come across immediately on video. It takes less skill to create the right tone, and it's more effective.

Disadvantages:

- Creating a video takes a little planning

Must-Do:

- As ever, do not forget your ideal customer profile and what your videos will do for them. You are not creating a video channel for general interest. This has to be aimed as always at your market.
- Don't forget the call to action!

You don't need to be a genius to see the power of video. How many people spent last night watching TV or other video, compared to reading a book? When you're searching for news items, what often comes up? When I wanted to know how to change a valve on my heating system, where did I look for a how-to?

Where do I look when I am searching for news articles?

When viewers share my video, do they just cut and paste a segment like with text, or do they link to my whole video and my YouTube channel?

What do teenagers spend hours of every day looking at?

YouTube is the answer to a lot of problems and it's no wonder it is so unbelievably massive.

Before I go on, I'll share something I can upon only a week or so ago in London. I was walking down the main shopping street, Oxford Street. Near the flagship Waterstones bookstore there were a couple of police vehicles and a mob of thousands of teenagers. There had been a book-signing that had been mobbed and gone completely out of control. 8,000 had turned up, and there were only 750 copies of the book. Most of the customers didn't even get inside the store, it was that bad. It was crazy.

Who was this superstar signing books? An actor? Singer? No. Rockstar? Sports star? No again. The super-popular author blocking Oxford Street with her crowds of fans was Zoe Suggs, a teenage video blogger or vlogger. That's the power of online video and YouTube.

Rather than go through the basics of getting on YouTube, I'll outline a six point plan for success with YouTube and video marketing.

The initial point is a repetition of what I have said before: if you want to create videos that connect with people, start with your Ideal Customer Profile. You must **create and share valuable video content that's relevant to what your ideal customer is searching for** on the Internet. That's your aim. And as before, it will work better, and you'll stick better to the plan, if you have a written plan.

Here's your generic ***Six Point Plan***

#1 *Answer the Questions* about your topic that people are asking. Your potential customers are going straight to Google to find answers to their questions. Claim your Google Authorship, then connect your Google+ profile with your YouTube channel and ***use video to deliver those answers***. You'll become a go-to Q&A resource in no time.

To get **ahead with the questions your customers ask most**, you will use keyword research tools, review forum questions or send out a survey to your existing subscribers and customers. Remember, content should be data-led. You are trying to score a direct hit when one of your customers makes a search on Google for a certain question, so do your research. No point answering the questions no one is asking! Use these questions to **create a library of question/solution videos that are short and to the point.** Provide real value, get to the point and go for the straight-talking image.

#2 *Use compelling and arresting research*, facts and stats that your customers will want to *share*. If your ideal customers want to share your material, you're winning, and of course sharing is one of the key functionalities of online media.

It's simple to make a slide with a chart or infographic which can be included in a voiced-over video. Present the research findings, include the source of the research for credibility, and then explain the significance in your own words, preferably with a video including yourself. This techniques creates shareable content, and it establishes your expertise since you are knowledgeable AND an analyst of the findings. What could be better?

#3 *Use a Trailer Video* to turn new viewers into subscribers.

The YouTube Trailer Video feature lets you **feature a video at the top of your channel when nonsubscribers visit**. Checkout this feature. It will let you create a "subscription-gate" where visitors are tempted to sign up because of the compelling content of your video. Of course you use your top video as bait and some powerful hooks in your short trailer to tempt them in.

You can use also use this space next to your trailer to **tell new viewers who you are**, what your business is all about and what they can expect from your content in general and your featured video in particular.

Your trailer video should be no more than 45-60 seconds. It should include:

> The Introduction —Welcome new viewers to your channel by introducing yourself and your business, then share notable credentials that will help instil confidence in the service you offer. Credentials should be "I have X years' experience and teach university classes at...", attributed testimonials or perhaps "I hold XX qualification and have helped hundreds to..."

> The Motivation—To captivate your audience, tell them what benefits they'll receive from your videos, then *share why you do what you do*. This personal story and your personal motivation is key to creating the all-important personal connection.

> The Call to Action—Wrap up your video and tell people *how to subscribe to your channel*. If you have a web page or blog you want them to visit, give them the URL.

#4: *Share a Customer Success Story to Establish a Good Reputation*. There are few things more powerful than a first-person testimonial that tells how your product or service made a customer's life better. In person, on video with a real person, this really comes alive.

This doesn't have to be polished and technical. You can **record customer interviews** with your mobile device or on a Google hangout with a simple webcam. Better if it's not too slick in fact. **Ask your best customers to put their own success stories** on camera and send you a link to their video so you can **share it on your own channel** and add it to your channel's favorites.

#5. ***Create a How-to Video Library.*** Similar to the answers-to-questions method, this should be backed up by keyword research into what people are looking for as how-tos.

The classics of this type are how-to videos like: "how to tile a bathroom wall" or "when and how to prune an apple tree". These are typically five-ten minutes long and give a methodical example of the technique. When it comes to business-type techniques, it is even easier to create compelling content using video screen capture software. "How to create a cashflow forecast" or "How to set up and register a new company in five minutes" can easily be done by talking the viewer through your screen captures. These videos are very immediate and empowering. Somehow a video makes people believe it is easy, where a step-by-step blog in written text would not.

Again, this is shareable content which is aimed squarely at Google's searches from your target market. It's vivid and makes your expertise come alive.

#6 *Don't forget the call to action!* If you're using a subscription-gate model, that can be your call to action. Otherwise mostly you'll be getting the visitors to your website to sign up to your email alerts and information.

It goes without saying that your video should be shared across Vimeo and DailyMotion and others and you should embed them in your site. Remember however that YouTube is highly integrated into Google and Google+ and that helps massively to get your video found by online searches.

Facebook

Advantages:

- Massive reach, especially with consumers
- Massive daily pageviews and stickiness
- Fantastic for sharing and generating buzz
- Facebook ads can be cost-effective
- Links extremely well into other Social Media such as YouTube and Amazon, meaning you can use Facebook to turbocharge your other Social Media activity with little effort
- Tools for polls, competitions and so on are built-in. It can be an effective web platform.
- Great for comments, conversations and feedback

- Especially effective for sharing images and videos virally
- A fantastic platform for generating immediate feedback and discussion. Excellent interaction with customers
- Conversation style allows your personality to come through
- Cheap to use

Disadvantages:

- Not so effective for business-to-business
- Can be confusing to users
- Time-consuming to use well
- Transient – nothing lasts very long
- So easy to waste time if you become distracted...

Must-Do:

- Research the platform
- Make a written plan
- Stick to the written plan and do not get distracted!

Facebook is the Big Daddy in terms of its reach online. Facebook is second only to YouTube in the number of searches it attracts, and Facebook has a titanic number of pageviews. In terms of active users it is second only to Google.

Facebook is essentially a visual network, for sharing images and videos. That's what works best. It encourages all sorts of comments and conversations, but getting noticed is mainly about getting your images and videos shared.

Because of its size, businesses cannot ignore Facebook as part of their marketing strategy. It will cost you time and a little money, and it's not perfect for attracting business customers - but it's huge.

The figures suggest that marketers believe Facebook is less effective at generating business leads than some other media. That may be because it can be complicated to get the best out of this platform. Put simply, Facebook offers so many options, and that can make it difficult. Youtube is simple and focused by comparison.

I do not claim to be a Facebook expert, so here are ten techniques from the experts. They are quite eye-opening. For more details and specific suggestions on these techniques, please see:

www.TheAttentionBusiness.com

These are tips from top Facebook brand managers. You'll see what I mean as it goes on.

1. Stay on topic

"People who Like your brand on Facebook expect your posts to be at least somewhat related to your brand or industry. Keeping your focus so narrow may seem limiting, especially if you're the one crafting the posts each day. Instead, ***think of it as a creative*** *challenge*," says Daniel Sundin, community manager at PETCO.

"Remember, Unliking a page is just as easy as Liking it. A single odd or off-topic post could get you booted from the stream," said Sundin.

I agree. It's so easy to get off topic with Facebook, but remember – you are targeting your ideal customer profile. Make that your lode star.

2. Ask the Right Questions of Friends and Fans

"One of the best ways to **get your fans talking on Facebook** is to ask interesting and entertaining questions. But did you know there's a right way and wrong way to ask questions on Facebook? When done right, you can significantly increase your fan engagement and build some great relationships," says Amy Porterfield, co-author of *Facebook Marketing All-In-One for Dummies*.

"Remember, people LOVE to talk about themselves, so when you make it about them, they are more likely to jump into the conversation," added Porterfield.

What's your pet-hate in business?

What's your favourite takeaway food?

What's the last concert you went to?

What's the worst service you ever had in a restaurant?

Remember, if you can keep the topic related to your business it's much better.

3. Include Pictures in Your Posts

"Twitter is a world of links, whereas Facebook is a picture economy. ***So just about every status update should include a picture***," says Guy Kawasaki, author of *Enchantment: The Art of Changing Hearts, Minds, and Actions.*

Pictures, videos... that's what Facebook thrives on.

4. Think "Club", not "List"

In fact this is a good approach across all of Social Media marketing.

In traditional marketing, were are used to thinking about lists, and of course you will need lists: email list, mailing lists, prospect lists etc. But Social Media marketing operates more like a club or a group of friends.

"Your Facebook audience is a club, not just a list, and you cannot satisfy the intellectual and sociological cravings of a club through one pithy status update each day," says Jay Baer, author of *The Now Revolution.*

I concur with Jay. Love Yourself, Love What You Do, and **Spread the Love!** Remember, these people are already your fans, so love them and treat them as friends!

5. Facebook Contests

"Everyone loves a contest and a chance to win. If you need a little excitement on your Facebook page, a contest will **spur your community to action**. Hopefully you will also get the benefit of people sharing your contest with their friends," says Andrea Vahl, co-author of *Facebook Marketing All-In-One for Dummies*.

"If you give away something your audience is interested in, you will **create great buzz for you and your Facebook page**," says Vahl.

There are a number of options and specific tools for making this work. Again, more detailed information to download at:

www.TheAttentionBusiness.com

6. Use Facebook as a Network

It's a network, right? In fact Facebook is The Network. That's the biggest plus point for Facebook, so use it. Make use of Facebook and *get instant feedback, ideas on new product design, how to market better and what topics are trending with your audience.*

Some marketers are reacting to Social Media, but smart marketers are **proactively** using Social Media to drive their business into new services and new directions. Use your Facebook conversations for market research and for ideas.

7. Measure your Facebook Marketing!

The need to measure applies to all marketing of course. If you can't measure effectiveness in some way or other, how do you know if you're doing the right thing?

8. Create a Calendar and Schedule for Your Facebook Marketing Activity

Keep it regular. Keep it going. Make it count. That means putting in the effort to make a planned programme of activity. This should tie in with your written Social Media plan. This is the detail of the written strategy, but make sure it always ties back in to your business case and your ideal customer.

Scheduling what you are going to do in terms of Facebook marketing has a number of plus points. In fact it's essential.

- It means you'll keep it up, even when you're busy.
- It means the quality of your work will be better, because it is preplanned rather than done "last minute".
- It means you'll control the mix of what you're doing on Facebook.
- It will fit in better with your other marketing work, offers etc.
- Hitting targets for the month demands marketing impact throughout the month, not just at monthend. Facebook can help you with this.
- You can pre-prepare your material all in one go, rather than doing it every day.
- Regular contact feels much better for your "club" of Facebook friends and fans.

Content creation is at the heart of this. It points visitors at your content, rather than away from your page to someone else's content.

9. Use the Happiness Index and Work with It

"Facebook has a Happiness Index that shows a spike of 10% on Fridays. As a marketer, you can take advantage of this increase in sentiment by doing something creative," says Mari Smith, co-author of *Facebook Marketing: An Hour a Day*.

"About once a month, I host 'Facebook Friday' (similar to #followfriday on Twitter), where I **invite all my fans to promote their own pages**, links to their blogs, Twitter, LinkedIn, Google+, etc. In addition, I know from other studies—and from my own fan page reports from PageLever —that my fans respond best to photos.

"By giving your fans specific times to cross-promote, network and create more visibility for their own pages, they'll be less inclined to do so outside of these windows, plus you'll **elevate your leadership and increase your news feed optimization**," said Smith.

You don't have to do exactly this, but think about the best times of the weeks for your customers when you're planning your calendar.

10. Try Out Sponsored Stories

"Facebook introduced a form of advertising called Sponsored Stories. These ads display activity from your friends in a fixed ad position on the page," says Ben Pickering, CEO of Strutta.

For example, if I Like your page, use your app or check in at your location, you can display an ad to all of my friends sharing that activity.

"Why would you pay to have something that is already in the news feed for free?"

- First, because the volume of activity in the feed can easily overwhelm any one update.
- Secondly, and of particular importance to those running apps on their page, is the fact that stories published from an app are subject to user feedback.

LinkedIn

Advantages:

- LinkedIn is seen as THE online platform for business- to-business networking. Of B2B online marketers, 98% are using LinkedIn
- Which also means there are very high levels of participation. Plenty of people in business see Facebook or Twitter as time-wasters, and many block these sites from their firewalls. Almost everyone in business is on LinkedIn
- Low-cost
- You can leverage both corporate and personal participation, getting employees to amplify the corporate message
- LinkedIn is excellent for reaching key decision makers
- LinkedIn is a great way to establish personal/company credibility. It gives you recommendations and a deep backstory which you can control

Disadvantages

- LinkedIn is a business-to-business medium/network, which means it's not for business-to-consumer

- It does not have the rapid, open conversations and feedback of Facebook. It's less useful for product testing and development
- LinkedIn is a long-term, strategic medium

Must-Do

- Long-term strategic plan and stick to it
- Create a network aimed at your target customers
- Work on your profile and image – it won't happen on its own

OK, so given the longer term benefits of Linkedin, you need to develop a strategy plan, and you need to stick to it. Sticking to the plan is of course, the crux of the matter, so let's look at the six points of your plan for long-term sustained success with Linkedin Marketing.

It doesn't matter if you're a large corporate brand or a small business, you can build a comprehensive LinkedIn marketing strategy on a scale that suits your needs and objectives.

#1. *Assess Your Resources* – This is a long-term commitment remember, so read through your options in this outline and think what it's going to mean for your business in terms of time, manpower and money. Companies big and small can make a success of this, but if don't have the resources, restrict your operations to only part of the plan. It's better to have a really solid platform and then expand if you can. Your platform begins with a really good LinkedIn company page.

#2: Build a First Class Company Page on LinkedIn

To create a business presence on LinkedIn and gain access to additional features that enhance your visibility, you must build a LinkedIn company page, and make sure it's optimized to be found by searches on LinkedIn itself and Google.

There's more on LinkedIn optimization on www.TheAttentionBusiness.com

Think of your LinkedIn company page as an *extension of your business website within LinkedIn*. Logos, infographics, products and services – it's all good. This is of course where the concept of re-use and repurposing is such an advantage. Everytime you create compelling, arresting and impressive material, you can use it again and again.

Invite existing employees, clients or customers, vendors and partners to follow your page, and showcase it to relevant LinkedIn members by using LinkedIn's paid targeted advertising.

www.linkedin.com/ads

Ask key clients or customers to recommend your products and services on your LinkedIn company page. These recommendations show up on your page for everyone to see, and serve as powerful testimonials for your business.

Filling your LinkedIn company page with compelling and interesting status updates requires ongoing work and effort, but it does work. If you have the resources for this, then do it.

As with the rest of Social Media, the best ways to gain authority and be impressive on LinkedIn are:

- Fill your profile with great content – browse other companies, see which ones you find impressive, then try to emulate and outdo them.
- Gain followers
- Gain recommendations – there is nothing wrong in asking for these from happy customers.

#3: Launch a LinkedIn Group Based on Your Company or Industry

LinkedIn groups are still going strong and are another component of a comprehensive strategy that helps position your company as an industry thought leader – see below. This is more work of course, and more work again to maintain, so skip this if you don't feel it's the best use of your time.

The most successful groups *focus on gaining relevant members with common goals*, and they are managed very well. It's like starting an interest group or a club for a hobby or an interest. It gives you credibility and you get to control it! But that means you have to do a good job, because if you don't, it kills your credibility instead. To implement a successful LinkedIn group strategy, assign the role of primary group manager/moderator to someone who pre-approves discussion posts, asks great questions and determines which members get accepted into the group.

When you launch your LinkedIn group, in the first place you'll need to get the word out organically to clients and customers, vendors, partners and influencers in your industry – and of course employees if you have them. *** This shows what a task the Linkedin Group can become. Do not take this on lightly.***

Identify top influencers and have them serve as group ambassadors to help recruit members and to lead interesting discussions to keep your group active.

Examples of corporate LinkedIn groups include these firms which have used the groups to aim at their target markets: Intuit (small business group), Staples (small business network) and Capital One (business traveler network). However, when you look through these, you'll see how much work is involved, so be careful what you commit to.

To help you **keep track of member demographics, growth and activity**, stats are available for all public LinkedIn groups.

#4: Work on a Thought Leadership Programme

Thought leadership is a buzzword which means drawing attention to stats and facts, asking key questions in your sector and answering some of those questions, as well as getting key influencers to give their own answers. Again, this is a lot of work, but the important thing is that thought leadership allows you to set the agenda, get press coverage, and get listened to.

Clearly, if everyone from your company is involved on LinkedIn, it creates an extended network that amplifies your company's message on this platform. That's a good thing. However, it means that all employees must be on message and following the same agenda, otherwise it kills your credibility.

This probably requires some degree of training in LinkedIn for employees, which is another commitment of resources.

#5: Paid LinkedIn Content Ads and Sponsored Updates

These are an expensive option, so you would only go down this road if you had a very good reason and if you had a full plan to test ad effectiveness upfront, and then to exploit the results with dedicated landing pages. It's possible recruitment companies and others for whom LinkedIn is a key resource could benefit.

While LinkedIn *social* ads grow company page followers and group membership, there are additional paid ads which run on LinkedIn that drive clicks to your website, or preferably to a specified landing page.

Do test your ad effectiveness upfront with taster campaigns, and monitor effectiveness during and afterwards. Self-service analytics tools can be found at:

http://partner.linkedin.com/ads/info/Ads_faqs_up dated_en_US.html

You will have noticed banner ads on LinkedIn that are designed to have members click through to company websites. Unfortunately, many times there's no specific call to action on the landing page! This is an elementary mistake. The same principles apply in LinkedIn as elsewhere:

- Target content to your ideal customer profile
- Identify your MDIs for the campaign
- Make a written plan
- Gently ease visitors to a Call to Action (to follow your page at least)
- Measure and monitor, especially for paid campaigns

#6: Monitor, Track, Adjust

If you're going to invest time and money in this, you're going to have business goals for what you're doing. These could be:

- **Increase your company's position** as a leader in your sector
- **Grow awareness, engagement and reach**

146

- **Generate qualified leads**

These can be touchy-feely, so do not forget to give yourself key performance metrics and deadlines, in terms of leads generated and converted, but also pageviews, followers and so on. Do not forget to track the number of visitors passed to your own site by LinkedIn.

LinkedIn is a fantastic network and resource, but if you followed the whole plan, it can soak up so much effort and time. Remember, whatever you do, you should do it well. If LinkedIn is not appropriate, don't use it. And if you can't commit to Groups and thought leadership, then again don't do it – just concentrate on building a first class company page on LinkedIn.

The Power of LinkedIn Connections

I heard recently about a businesswoman who wanted an "in" to the education market in a certain Caribbean state. She did not know the right civil servant in that country, or even their name, and she had no way of contacting.

However, by running some searches on LinkedIn, she was able to find and message someone in a related job position who knew the chief of education in that territory. That contact was happy to correspond, and quickly passed on the contact details for the chief of education. Within a day or so, my contact was able to get email address, phone number and some background information on a key prospect four thousand miles away. That's the power of LinkedIn.

An Interlude: "Offline Social Media"

As I have mentioned, I have done some work with travel businesses, mainly creating marketing plans. They do face some particular problems in that they tend to be cash-negative, and they face intense competition from the huge online sellers.

Sandra and Dave recently asked me to a make an online and Social Media marketing plan for their independent travel agency. I went ahead and created the plan, and they were surprised that I had gone so heavily for *offline* activities in the plan.

Small businesses, both local and national, need to embed themselves in their communities of target customers. The point of online media and online Social Media is to make it ***cheap and easier*** to network and embed your personality and your business in these target communities. Usually, it is vastly cheaper and easier.

However, face-to-face networking and participation in events, shows and conferences have some major advantages:

- They are excellent market research. You really get a feel for what people want, what they need and what irritates them. You gain this feeling very quickly.

148

- They create goodwill. You are no longer a faceless, profit-driven seller – you are part of the community, and participating. You are helping and joining in.

The online activity and Social Media back up this activity and run alongside. They also work 24/7, which is cool.

When I made that plan for Sandra and Dave, I reminded them that they were asking families to spend thousands with them. That requires trust in a brand new company, which could fail even before the holiday comes around! Fortunately, both are well connected locally through church and schools. They are already trusted by the circle who know them. The aim of their marketing plan is to extend that circle of trust to more and more people in the locality, and am I am glad to say that their commitment to the offline part of the plan - community events, backed up by embedding themselves in local directories, Google Local and more - has really worked.

Sandra and Dave's agency is unlikely to always be the cheapest option, but customers trust them. They have done well. Conversely, Sandra was telling me about two guys who set up an agency at about the same time in a different city. They have concentrated on online-only, and it has not worked nearly as well, because customers have not been able to put names to faces. Consequently they are always competing on price alone.

I had a similar experience when I was running my business selling technical computing books. My target market was programmers, software developers and IT professionals. Our business was mostly online as you can imagine. Nonetheless, we embedded ourselves not only in the online hangouts of our target customers, but also made an effort to meet face-to-face.

We attended dozens of user group meetings, confererences and seminars each year, from 30-40 attendees, right up to national events with thousands. We partnered and we helped out and supported. The goodwill was immense, and it helped us compete with Amazon. We still had to be competitive on price and service of course, but all this activity put us top of mind.

'You're everywhere,' a programmer said to me at one conference. That was so gratifying, because our budget and our margins were so small, and there were only five of us in the business. In truth we *were* everywhere, online and off, for that community. But for a niche target market, everywhere is not necessarily that big.

Resources permitting, that should be your aim – to be everywhere, online and off, for your target customers. It may not be possible, but especially for local businesses, it's a great concept to think about.

The Internet means you can be on their phone, on their desktop, on their TV, on their tablet... but if you have the opportunity to speak to them face to face, don't pass it up.

If you've targeted well, "everywhere" may not be all that big.

Twitter

Advantages:

- Quick to set up, quick to post
- Very immediate
- A broadcast medium
- Very effective for personal and personality-based offerings
- You can ride trending topics to get seen
- Retweet is an easy sharing system that can get you in front of thousands of eyeballs
- Spontaneous and spur of the moment
- Good for conversations
- Great for responding to breaking news

Disadvantages:

- Too easy to set up and post. Noise level is huge
- Messages are transient and have a currency of minutes
- Time-consuming
- Difficult to create a proper profile in 140 characters

Twitter is a tough platform to do well with. Whereas most of the other platforms online give the opportunity for you to grab attention and inform using a carefully crafted profile, Twitter gives you 140 characters for each message and 140 characters for your profile, plus a couple of images and a space for your web address.

Furthermore, because it takes so little effort to get involved with Twitter, it seems as if half the world is tweeting at once. It can feel as though you're in an aircraft hangar with 5000 others, and everyone is shouting, while no one is listening.

These problems are caused mainly, as ever, by lack of planning and by not focusing on what you are trying to achieve, and what Twitter is good for.

Twitter is best for personal comments and for a personality-based identity. The witty, pithy personalities are always popular on Twitter. Quick, hilarious reactions to breaking news and sports events work extremely well.

Dare I say that not every company's persona fits all that well with this? Twitter can be used in other ways of course, but it's worth bearing that in mind when choosing whether or not to engage in Twitter.

Perhaps the best way to make your decision on whether or not to tweet is to go through some dos and don'ts and see how you could perform.

DO tweet regularly. A good rule of thumb is 10-15 times a day and much more if you get into conversations. Half of these should be retweets.

DO check out breaking news, trending topics and hot topics, and tweet around them. This will generate far more traffic.

DO use Twitter to bring visitors to your blog or your site, but be sure you have a good hook, ie "#Free", "5 Ways to...", "The 10 Secrets of..." etc

DO make your tweets retweetable. The real action is in getting retweeted, so give them a reason to retweet, and do plenty of retweeting so that people return the favour

DO look for opportunities to be funny or witty and to use funny images etc

DON'T forget to target your ideal customers. These will often be harder to target than general industry stakeholders, but remember that is what you are here for.

DO make the best use of your profile and the images you are allowed.

DO use trackable URL's in your Tweets, via Bit.ly for instance, so you can monitor the effectiveness of your work.

DO make a plan and stick with it. This essentially means preparing a bunch of tweets ahead of time and scheduling them in, using a piece of software which will let you schedule, such as Tweetdeck or Hootsuite. The idea is to mix in these pre-prepared messages with your spur-of-the-moment-tweets. This planning will keep your tweeting more on message and fight against the drift of random tweeting at all times of the day or night.

DON'T have private conversations over Twitter – "See you later in the Red Lion". It turns your followers off.

DO Tweet answers to problems and questions with links to your site and videos

DON'T push your company and your products down their throats. One in ten tweets maximum should be about your products and services.

DON'T Tweet for the sake of it...

The last point there pretty much spells out the problem with Twitter. You need some really good stuff to tweet about, and you need to do it 5-10 times a day! That's a lot and it's so easy to let the quality drop. Then you should only tweet once or twice a day about products and services. What do you fill the rest with besides retweets? The proper answer is that you are bang up to date on breaking news and putting out your angle and view on it all. This is all very well, but who has the time to stay glued to Twitter? It's tough.

In a nutshell, Twitter is harder than it looks. With Facebook, LinkedIn, Amazon, YouTube and Google, you can use mostly perspiration and a little inspiration to succeed. Twitter by contrast demands a lot of inspiration to do it well.

If you're keen, there is a great article at my site about building a strong Twitter following:

www.theattentionbusiness.com

Amazon – as a Social Medium

Amazon is clearly an amazing online platform for selling goods and gaining visibility. Amazon practically does everything for you!

This is NOT what this chapter, or this book, is about; but here are some of the advantages of Amazon as a selling platform.

- Amazon showcases your goods, collects the money, takes away the credit card fraud risk and pays you promptly.
- Amazon will warehouse your stock for a low fee.

- Amazon's delivery services may well offer better rates than you could find for yourself
- You use the power of Amazon customer reviews
- You benefit from the seeing the sales rank of every item on there! This is an astonishing market research tool.
- If you're on Amazon Marketplace you can gain access to Amazon's stock list including current prices and availability. This is unbelievable.
- The huge server space offered by Amazon Web Services is laughably cheap and you can start using it in well under an hour.

Honestly, I ran a niche-targeted online seller of books and training for a number of years. I competed that whole time with Amazon. I KNOW how good Amazon is as a selling platform.

However, I am going to tell you now about the other side of Amazon, which ties into your Social Media work and is such a powerful tool in building brand your brand, reputation and credibility. This technique compliments your content and online strategy, and can really open doors for you into the bargain.

Advantages:

- Excellent for branding and credibility
- Very good for knowledge-based service businesses, such as lawyers, accountants, financial services, real estate, advisors, consultants, designers, technical businesses etc

- Offers easy and eye-catching ways of grabbing the attention of key players
- Ties right in with your content creation and reuse strategy
- Excellent response to online searches
- Can be used in offline situations also
- After the initial hard work, this forms a lasting resource which won't take a lot of effort
- Opens doors for press articles
- Opens doors for public speaking opportunities
- You actually get paid for doing it

Disadvantages:

- This can be a lot of work initially, and it can be daunting
- You might not want to write a book – see below
- You won't get rich from book sales alone – that's not the point

I refer of course to the "book is the new business card" opportunity which Amazon now offers.

Not many years ago, if you wanted to write a book, it was a very daunting undertaking. You firstly had to write a book and find an editor, while pretty much guessing what the popular topics and titles would be. Secondly, you had to finance the printing of the book. Thirdly, you or the publisher had to use a distribution network and persuade all the bookstores to carry the book in stock. Then, if the books in the stores didn't sell, you could expect to get them all sent back from the shops for a full refund.

In truth, it was even worse than this simplified version. Suffice to say, it was a risky, costly venture, and the writing of the work was only a minor part of the problem.

The advent of ebooks, print-on-demand and the Amazon platform have changed all that.

You can publish an ebook on Amazon Kindle, create a hard-copy version for sale through Amazon's CreateSpace and have your books listed and sold on the world's best sales platform for no financial outlay at all! You can even offer your Kindle book for free to get thousands of copies out there, and take advantage of Kindle Unlimited which will make your book available for free lending.

So getting a book out there and distributing it has become way, way easier. Great. So what's the big deal about books?

Firstly, 90% of non-fiction books are written by experts and authorities in their field. Turning up to any pitch, or meeting or networking event with your own book confers MASSIVE credibility. Being an author creates respect, credibility and gravitas the instant you hold up that book.

You can use Amazon to send a gift-wrapped copy to an important prospect or client. Who does NOT open a parcel from Amazon? Which PA would open that for his or her boss? A book can open doors.

You can list the book on your website and link to it. You can use it on your publicity.

You can use the material from the book for innumerable blog posts, Facebook posts, Google optimization etc etc.

You can list the book on your CV/resume and LinkedIn page.

You can use the book as an instant reference to gain public speaking opportunities and interviews/articles for journalists.

Most importantly, the book on a topic in your chosen field gives you a rarity value straight away. It puts you a cut above. It is a distinguishing factor.

And then... there is the opportunity for Amazon to send traffic back to your website! You can expound your thoughts and considered opinions on your topic and show the readers how to solve their problems. Since there is no way that readers want every last detail of the how-tos, you should be pointing them towards extra material and how-to videos on your website.

You can see that this is quite a sophisticated integrated approach to information sharing and creating connections. If you or your team are working on content creation, you're already doing most of the work! Perhaps more than any other technique in Social Media Marketing, this technique shows that the Internet Giants want you and your knowledge and your expertise. Amazon, Google, Facebook, YouTube, LinkedIn – they are nothing without people like you who have specific skills and knowledge to offer.

It also shows vividly why The Attention Business of Social Media Marketing is really **show business**. You have the knowledge and the ideas and the know-how. Social Media marketing is about **packaging** that knowledge and showing it to best advantage. You have the knowledge. You need only to package it and share it, in multiple versions, again and again.

Here are some of the extra benefits of creating a book on Amazon and leveraging your knowledge and skills:

- Show yourself off to a massive audience, filtered down to exactly those readers who are looking for the knowledge you have to share.
- Access individuals who are specifically looking for knowledge who would never use Facebook or Twitter.
- Just as some consumers would never read a book, plenty of people would never look on YouTube for guidance. Those people like books.
- Reading a book is a very personal thing and it gets your know-how deep inside people's heads.
- A book is about more than a how-to – it shows off a way of thinking and a deeper understanding of the subject. A 5 minute video does not do that.
- A book can effectively be a gentle, low-pressure selling tool for your business – but, of course, you can't be pushy.
- Amazon lets you make your book free for five days a quarter. If you promote the book at these times, you can achieve thousands of downloads with readers who never knew you existed.

- The books are a low-cost giveaway, either in exchange for email addresses or filling in a survey on your site, or in exchange for business cards at an event, as prizes in a competition and so on.
- When you are using your books to promote your business, you know you are **always** dealing with qualified, interested leads.
- The book brings your information and your thinking together and packages it up.

Cool.

I almost have you convinced. It's all good. ***But...***

It's a big "but". Not everyone wants to sit down and write a book. I understand that. I enjoy writing and so do many others, but I struggle to find the time. For most small business owners, this will sound like a non-starter, an impossibility. Some will even say they don't have enough knowledge to write a book like this. My advice, however, would be that this is nothing like as difficult as it sounds. No one wants to read a huge book. For business topics especially, they like them short and to-the-point. 15,000-20,000 words are fine, and you should try not to go over 30,000.

There is a process you should follow, which I share in more detail on www.theattentionbusiness.com, and as ever you should begin with the "what" rather than the "how" of this task. "What" means your subject matter and title. Think about what your ideal customers really want, what titles would hook them in, and what problems they really want answered. There are ways you can validate your choice of title and subject on Amazon.com.

It's important to validate your "what" before you start writing, and even before you start planning the book. You'll see what I mean by checking the info sheet I have put online. Validating your subject matter and areas of focus like this will help you home right in on what you need to do.

Concentrate on inspiration, insights and information, *in that order*. Readers are looking for your personal insights and how they will make things easier and more successful. Without inspiration about how you can empower them, why should your readers read at all?

Again, to help focus your subject matter, take the project in this order:

1. Choose a subject related to your business which you love and are passionate about.
2. Check on Amazon to see which titles sell best in this subject area.
3. Throw around some ideas for interesting and enticing titles.
4. Write a promo piece for your book, explaining to the audience why they simply *have to read* this, and what it will do for them. Give it as many enticing hooks as you can.
5. Plan out your book, based in the promo piece you just wrote. Yes, the promo piece should come before the writing. It is key to your planning.

6. Write the book, or engage someone to write the book for you. If it is a professional writer, you can give interviews, or record questions and answers by voice to help the writer.
7. Make sure there are links and references to your site and your business throughout the book.
8. If doing the work yourself, you can still dictate out the material and then hand it to an editor. You'll find tons of good editorial services on Elance or Peopleperhour.
9. When the book is written, print it off, read carefully and correct yourself with a pen.
10. Get another proof reader to check and correct.
11. Engage a professional designer for the cover.

In terms of producing a professional product, the proofreading for errors in the English and the quality of the cover are paramount.

Again, there is much more detail about this on www.TheAttentionBusiness.com.

Email – (Still) The Internet's Killer App

Some of us will remember, way back before Tim Berners-Lee developed http and hyperlinks and launched the World Wide Web, that the Internet was already in common use.

That's right. Before the Web existed, millions of business people were already paying for their clunky, slow Internet connections, because they were essential for business. Business folk were coughing up money for their Compuserve accounts well before anyone had even seen a website, and certainly before anyone had thought of the concept of a search engine to find the sites.

Why was this?

Email is the answer. The Internet's first killer app. You could communicate instantaneously, and you could even send quite large documents around the world. It's unbelievably useful.

Now, email marketing has been debased by spam over the years. Fatigue with the scams and unwanted junk has made it easy for marketers to dismiss the idea of email marketing in favour of Social Media especially.

But... Let me ask you one thing. Does Facebook use email? Does Twitter use email? What about all the other Giants of the Internet. Do they use email? They most certainly do.

The fact is, email is still the easiest and most powerful way of getting your customers and prospects to engage - even if that means getting them to read your blog, or follow you on Twitter or join your Facebook contest. And for other offers and events you might plan it's invaluable. Email, even now, is still the Internet's Killer Marketing App.

Gathering email addresses is still ABSOLUTELY CRITICAL to modern marketing. Do not neglect this simple but essential task. Find yourself simple and effective ways of gathering those email addresses and get on with it.

More Detail and Specifics – Guides, Tools, Checklists and Resources to Download

There are already over 20 articles, guides, blogs and info sheets to go with this book (at time of writing) with more being added all the time.

www.TheAttentionBusiness.com

Including the following downloads:

<u>Four Steps to Success with Organic Search Optimization and Marketing</u>

This 42 page guide gives you step by step guidance, sometimes in close technical detail, of what you need to do to make sure your site is:

- Scanned regularly by Google
- Given a great index entry on the search engine
- Ranked as well as possible in the PageRank system
- Shown on the Google search results in a way that entices visitors to click through

<u>The Public Relations and Press Coverage Plan for Profit</u>

A nine page guide on the power of free press coverage, online and offline.

- How PR can bring in thousands, very quickly

- Four essentials when presenting yourself to the press
- What to put in a great press release
- 10 winning ideas for press releases and coverage
- What the journalist will do, and what you must do

How to Write Powerful Marketing Emails

20 page guide on the principles and practice of writing emails that work

- Essential tools
- Dos and don'ts
- Tips and techniques
- Technical details

Secrets of Long-Tail Search Engine Marketing

A 7 page guide on why long-tail search marketing is so effective for both paid (Adwords) search marketing, and organic search marketing.

- Gain access to the forgotten hordes of Internet searchers
- Address their problem directly
- Increase traffic and increase your conversion rates at the same time

The Best Keyword Research Tools

A 4 page review of the best keyword research tools and what each is good for. We all know that all your social media and content MUST be underpinned by quantitative work on what customers search for. These tools are the perfect way to do that.

The Best Social Media Automation Tools

7 pages of unbiased, detailed, practical reviews. You'd be mad not to automate as much as you can of the social media "grunt work". You need to leave yourself free to create content, add value and network, and let the machines do the heavy lifting of getting your stuff as widely distributed as possible. Automation tools are a key way of reducing overwhelm and executing an effective plan.

Strategy Plan Template for Social Media Marketing

A nine page, nine step template plan you can run off and use straight away. Includes detailed explanations and suggestions. Everyone knows that having a plan is a good idea, but it's hard to dream one up from scratch.

- Where to start
- How to make it as easy as you can
- Great ideas for posts and content creation
- Which parts of the plan you can skip, and which are essential
- Plan to maximise traffic and awareness for the least effort

Effective Branding for Digital Marketers

A 7 page guide on how to define and establish a brand online

- Why even small businesses need a brand online
- Multiple checklists and step-by-step how-tos of how define and create your brand
- How to maintain consistency
- How to target correctly
- What is branding on digital platform

Ten Ways to Increase Sales This Month with Social Media Marketing

9 pages. A hard-hitting report on steps you can take right now to beat your month's targets.

So much of digital marketing is medium- to long-term. These are techniques that you can use right now to boost traffic, leads and sales.

To Outsource (5 Reasons), or Not To Outsource (4 Reasons)

5 page hard-hitting report.

- Five reasons not to do digital marketing yourself
- Four reasons to be wary of outsourcing

www.TheAttentionBusiness.com

Thankyou for reading.

■ ✍